MADHUR JAFFREY'S
INDIAN
COOKERY

MADHUR JAFFREY'S

INDIAN
COOKERY

CONTENTS

Page 1: View from the Taj Mahal at sunset
Pages 2 & 3: From the left: Plain basmati rice,
Tomato, onion and green coriander relish,
Cauliflower with potatoes, Prawns in a sauce

Madhur Jaffrey's Indian Cookery was first published by the British Broadcasting Corporation in 1982

© Madhur Jaffrey 1982

This newly illustrated, slightly abridged edition has been published by arrangement with BBC Enterprises Limited in 1989 by The Hamlyn Publishing Group, a division of the Octopus Publishing Group, Michelin House, 81 Fulham Road, London SW3 6RB

Design and illustrations (except where credited) © Hennerwood Publications Limited 1986

ISBN 0 600 56363 4

Produced by Mandarin Offset
Printed and bound in Hong Kong

INTRODUCTION

I HAVE ALWAYS loved to eat well. My mother once informed me that my passion dates back to the hour of my birth when my grandmother wrote the sacred syllable 'Om' ('I am') on my tongue with a finger dipped in fresh honey. I was apparently observed smacking my lips rather loudly.

Starting from that time, food – good food – just appeared miraculously from somewhere at the back of our house in Delhi. It would be preceded by the most tantalizing odours – steaming basmati rice, roasting cumin seeds, cinnamon sticks in hot oil – and the sounds of crockery and cutlery on the move. A bearer, turbaned, sashed and barefooted, would announce the meal and soon we would all be sitting around the dinner table, a family of six, eating monsoon mushrooms cooked with coriander and turmeric, *rahu* fish that my brothers had just caught in the Jamuna River and cubes of lamb smothered in a yogurt sauce.

It was at this stage of innocence that I left India for London, to become a student at the Royal Academy of Dramatic Art. My 'digs' were in Brent and consisted of a pleasant room and, through the kindness of my landlords, use of the kitchen.

'Use of the kitchen' was all very well, but

exactly *how* was I going to use it? My visits to our kitchen in Delhi had been brief and intermittent. I could not cook. What was worse, I felt clumsy and ignorant.

An SOS to my mother brought in return a series of reassuring letters, all filled with recipes of my favourite foods. There they were, *Kheema matar* (Minced meat with peas), *Rogan josh* (Red lamb stew), *Phool gobi aur aloo ki bhaji* (Cauliflower with potatoes) . . .

Slowly, aided by the correspondence course with my encouraging mother, I did learn to cook, eventually getting cocky enough to invite large groups of friends over for meals of *Shahi korma* (Royal lamb or beef with a creamy almond sauce) or *Shahjahani murghi* (Mughlai chicken with almonds and raisins). Once certain basic principles had been mastered, cooking Indian food had become perfectly accessible.

There is something so very satisfying about Indian cookery, more so when it is fresh and home-cooked. Perhaps it is that unique blending of herbs, spices, seasonings, as well as meat, pulses, vegetables, yogurt dishes and relishes that my ancestors determined centuries ago would titillate our palates. At the same time it preserves our health and the proper chemical balance of our bodies. This combination of wholesome food and endless flavours and dishes makes Indian cookery one of the greatest in the world.

Indian food is far more varied than the menus of Indian restaurants suggest. One of my fondest memories of school in Delhi is of the lunches that we all brought from our homes, ensconced in multi-tiered tiffin-carriers. My stainless steel tiffin-carrier used to dangle from the handles of my bicycle as I rode at great speed to school every morning, my ribboned pigtails fluttering behind me. The smells emanating from it sustained me as I dodged exhaust-spewing buses and later, as I struggled with mind-numbing algebra. When the lunch bell finally set us free, my friends and I would assemble under a shady *neem* tree if it was summer or on a sunny verandah if it was winter. My mouth would begin to water even before we opened up our tiffin-carriers. It so happened that all my friends were of differing faiths and all came, originally, from different regions of the country. Even though we were all Indian, we had hardly any culinary traditions in common. Eating always filled us with a sense of adventure and discovery as we could not always anticipate what the others might bring.

My Punjabi friend was of the Sikh faith. She often brought large, round parathas made with wheat and ghee produced on her family farm. These parathas were sometimes stuffed with tart pomegranate seeds and sometimes with cauliflower. We ate them with a sweet-and-sour homemade turnip pickle.

Another friend was a Muslim from Uttar Pradesh, known to bring beef cooked with spinach, deliciously flavoured with chillies, cardamom and cloves. Many of us were Hindus and not supposed to eat beef. So we just pretended not to know what it was. Our fingers would work busily around the tender meat that covered the bones and our cheeks would hollow as we sucked up the spicy marrow from the marrow bones. But we never asked what we were eating. The food was far too good for that. On the other hand, whenever my father went boar-hunting and we cooked that meat at home, I never took it to school. I knew it would offend my Muslim friends.

Another member of our gang was a Jain from Gujerat. Jains are vegetarians, some of them so orthodox as to refrain from eating beetroots and tomatoes because their colour reminds them of blood, and root vegetables because in pulling them out of the earth some innocent insect might have to lose its life. This friend occasionally brought the most delicious pancakes — pooras — made out of legumes.

One of us came from Kashmir, India's northernmost state. As she thrilled us with tales about tobogganing — the rest of us had never seen snow — she would unpack morel

The Red Fort, Delhi

7

mushrooms cooked with tomatoes and peas and flavoured with asafetida. She was a Hindu, of course. Only Kashmiri Hindus cook with asafetida. And they do not cook with garlic. Kashmiri Muslims cook with garlic and frown upon asafetida. I found all this much easier to follow than algebra.

We had a South Indian friend too, a Syrian Christian from Kerala. She often brought *idlis*, steamed rice cakes that we ate with *sambar*, a pulse and vegetable stew.

I, a Delhi Hindu, tried to dazzle my friends with quail and partridge which my father shot regularly and which our cook prepared with onions, ginger, cinnamon, black pepper and yogurt.

India is such a large country — over a million square miles of changing topography, divided into thirty-one states and territories. Geography and local produce have played a great part in forming regional culinary traditions. Religious groups within each state have modified these regional cuisines even further to suit their own restrictions. History too, has had its influences. Goa, for example, on India's west coast, was ruled by the Portuguese for four centuries. Many of its people were converted to Catholicism, some by Saint Francis Xavier himself, and eventually developed an eating style which included platters of Beef roulade — a stuffed roll of beef cooked in garlic-flavoured olive oil, and a dessert of layered pancakes — *bibingka* — made with egg yolks, coconut milk and raw Indian sugar. British colonialists left quite a few dishes in their wake too. There were those *cutlis* (cutlets) that our cook made. He, of course, marinated them in ginger and garlic first. Then, there was the strong influence of the Moghuls. They had come to India via Persia in the sixteenth century and introduced the sub-continent to delicate pullaos and meats cooked with yogurt and fried onions.

If there is a common denominator in all Indian foods, it is, perhaps, the imaginative use of spices. Does this mean that Indian food is always spicy? Well, in a sense it does. It always

View from Dal Lake, Srinagar, Kashmir

Spice market

uses spices, sometimes just one spice to cook a potato dish and sometimes up to fifteen spices to make an elaborate meat dish. But it is not always hot. The 'heat' in Indian food comes from hot chillies. Chilli peppers were introduced to Asia in the sixteenth century by the Portuguese who had discovered them in the New World. Our own pungent spices until that time were the more moderate mustard seeds and black peppercorns. Those of you who do not like hot food should just leave out all the chillies – red, green or cayenne – in my recipes. Your food will still be authentically Indian, superb in flavour and not at all hot.

The spices and seasonings that we *do* like to use in our food include cumin, coriander, turmeric, black pepper, mustard seeds, fennel seeds, cinnamon, cardamom and cloves. Sometimes we leave the spices whole and fry them, sometimes we roast the spices and at other times we grind them and mix them with water or vinegar to make a paste. Each of these techniques draws out a completely different flavour from the same spice. This way we can give a great variety to, say, a vegetable like a potato, not only by methods such as boiling, baking and roasting but by cooking it with whole cumin one time, a combination of ground cumin and roasted fennel another time, and black pepper a third time. The permutations become endless as does the possibility of variety in tastes. Does this mean that you cannot cook Indian food without having a whole lot of spices? I suggest that you start off with buying the specific spices you need to cook a selected dish and then slowly increase your spice 'wardrobe'. It is a bit like being a painter, I suppose. If you have a palette glowing with magenta and cobalt blue and sap green and vermilion, it will give you the confidence – and the choice – to do anything you want. You could use one colour, if you desired, or ten. It is the same with spices. It is nice to know that they are there. Whole spices last a long time. This way, you can cook aubergines with fennel seeds one day and green beans with cumin seeds the next day, if that is what you want.

Once you have mastered the use of Indian spices, you will find yourself not only cooking Indian meals but also inventing dishes with an Indian flavour and using Indian spices in unexpected ways. A French chef who once observed me cooking, now regularly uses ground roasted cumin seeds in his cream of tomato soup. I myself have created an Indian-style dish of pork chipolatas (page 40) for this book to start you off in this pleasant direction. Since it is the carefully orchestrated use of spices, seasonings and flavourings that gives Indian food its unique character, it might be useful to examine them singly and remove their mystery.

Spices, Seasonings and Flavourings

Dried
red
chilli

Weighing red
chillies, Udaipur,
Rajasthan

Cardamo
seeds

Green
chilli

Ground
cardamom

MANY OF THE spices used in Indian foods can now be found in supermarkets. These include cumin, coriander, turmeric, cloves, cinnamon, cardamom, nutmeg, black pepper, bay leaves, ginger, paprika and cayenne pepper. Others have to be searched out from delicatessens and Greek, Indian or Pakistani grocers. Such grocers can now be found in all major cities and many small towns as well. It is also possible to order spices by post.

Ideally speaking, it is best to buy all dry spices in their whole form. They will stay fresh for long periods if stored in cool, dry, dark places in tightly lidded jars. This way you can grind the spices as you need them. I use an electric coffee-grinder for this purpose although a pestle and mortar would do. The more freshly ground the spices, the better their flavour. If you can only buy ground spices, buy small quantities and store them, too, in cool, dry, dark places in tightly lidded jars.

When transferring spices from plastic packets to jars, be sure to label them. When buying spices from ethnic grocers, make sure that they are labelled. Many of my cooking students have come to me with unlabelled jars and asked, 'What do I have here?' Even I, who have been cooking now for twenty-five years, cannot tell the difference between ground cumin and ground coriander without tasting or smelling them first.

Here is a list of the spices, seasonings and flavourings I have used in this book:

Asafetida

Heeng

The Indian source for this smelly resin has traditionally been Afghanistan and Western Kashmir. In its lump form, asafetida looks rather like the brown rosin my husband uses on the bow of his violin. Its smell is another matter. James Beard, America's foremost food writer, once compared the smell to that of fresh

10

Green
ardamom

truffles. This seasoning is a digestive and is used in very small quantities. (It can even cure horses of indigestion!) A pinch of it is thrown into very hot oil and allowed to fry for a second before other foods are added. As asafetida can only be found at Indian and Pakistani grocers, I have made its use optional in my recipes. If you wish to purchase it, I suggest that you buy the smallest box available of *ground* asafetida. Make sure that the lid sits tightly on the box when you store it.

White
cardamom

Cardamom, pods and seeds

Elaichi

Cardamom pods are whitish or green and have parchment-like skins and lots of round, black, highly aromatic seeds inside. The whitish pods are more easily available in supermarkets. They have been bleached and have less flavour and aroma than the unbleached green ones. For my recipes, use whichever pods you can find easily, although the green ones are better. Many of my recipes call for whole pods. They are used as a flavouring in both savoury and sweet dishes. When used whole, cardamom pods are not meant to be eaten. We leave them on the side of the plate, along with any bones.

When a recipe calls for cardamom *seeds*, you can either take the seeds out of the pods (a somewhat tedious task, best done while watching television) or else you can buy the seeds from the few Indian and Pakistani grocers who sell them. If my recipe calls for a small amount of *ground* cardamom seed, just pulverize the seeds in a mortar.

ayenne
epper

Cayenne pepper

Pisi hui lal mirch

Made from dried red chillies, this is called red chilli powder by Indian and Pakistani grocers. Most of my recipes have a flexible amount of cayenne pepper in them. It is hard to know how hot people like their food. Use the smaller amount if you want your foods just mildly hot and the larger amount if you want it hotter. Cayenne pepper is sold in all supermarkets.

ardamom
eds

Chillies, fresh, hot, green

Hari mirch

These fresh chillies, 5-10 cm (2-4 inches) long, green outside and filled with flat, round white seeds, are sold by Asian grocers, some supermarkets and increasingly in street markets. Besides being rich in Vitamins A and C, they give Indian foods a very special flavour. If my recipe calls for them, make at least one good effort to find them. If you are unsuccessful, use a little more cayenne pepper as a substitute.

Green chillies should be stored unwashed and wrapped in newspaper, in a plastic container in the refrigerator. Any chillies that go bad should be thrown away as they affect the whole batch.

Important: Be careful when handling cut green chillies. Refrain from touching your eyes or your mouth; wash your hands as soon as possible, otherwise you will 'burn' your skin with the irritant the chillies contain. If you want the green chilli flavour without most of the heat, remove the white seeds.

Green
chilli

Cinnamon

Chillies, whole, dried, hot, red

Sabut lal mirch

These chillies, about 4-5 cm (1½-2 inches) long and about 1 cm (⅓-½ inch) wide, are often thrown into hot oil for a few seconds until they puff up and their skin darkens. This fried skin adds its own very special flavour to a host of meats, vegetables and pulses. Handle these chillies carefully, making sure that you wash your hands well before you touch your face. If you want the flavour of the chillies without their heat, make a small opening in them and then shake out and discard their seeds.

These chillies are sold by most Asian grocers and in many supermarkets.

Cinnamon

Dar cheeni

Buy sticks. We often use them whole in meat and rice dishes. The sticks are used just for their flavour and aroma and are not meant to be eaten. They can be found in all supermarkets.

Cloves, whole

Long

Cloves

We often use whole cloves in our meat and rice dishes for their flavour and aroma. They are not meant to be eaten. (It must be added that we do suck on cloves as a mouth freshener.) Whole cloves are sold by most supermarkets.

Coconut, fresh grated

Nariyal

Coconut

When buying coconuts, make sure that they are crack-free and have no mould on them. Shake them to make sure that they are heavy with liquid. Now hold a coconut in one hand over a sink and hit it around the centre with the claw end of a hammer or with the blunt side of a heavy cleaver. The coconut should crack and break into two halves. (You could, if you like, collect the liquid in a cup. It is not used in cooking, but you may drink it. I do. I consider it my reward for breaking open the coconut in the first place.) Taste a piece of the coconut to make sure it is sweet and not rancid. Prise off the coconut flesh from the hard shell with a knife. If it proves to be too obstinate, it helps to put the coconut halves, cut side up, directly over a low flame, turning them around now and then so they char slightly. The woody shell contracts and releases the kernel.

Now peel off the brown coconut skin with a potato peeler and break the flesh into 2.5 cm (1 inch) pieces (larger ones if you are grating manually). Wash these coconut pieces and either grate them finely on a hand grater or else put them in an electric blender or food processor. Do not worry about turning them into pulp in these electric machines. What you will end up with will be very finely 'grated' coconut, perfect for all the Indian dishes that require it.

Grated coconut freezes beautifully and thaws fast. I always grate large quantities whenever I have the time and store it in the freezer for future use.

Fresh coconuts are sold by all Asian grocers and are widely available in ordinary greengrocers' shops.

Coriander, fresh green

Hara dhaniya or kothmir

Coriander seeds

This is one of India's favourite herbs and is used, just as parsley might be, both as a garnish and for its flavour. This pretty green plant grows about 15-20 cm (6-8 inches) in height. Just the top, leafy section is used, though the stems are sometimes thrown into pulse dishes for their aroma. This herb is worth hunting for as its delicate flavour is unique. It is sold by Asian grocers, but it may also be grown at home from coriander seeds.

Fresh coriander

To store fresh green coriander, put it in its unwashed state, roots and all, into a container filled with water, almost as if you were putting flowers in a vase. The leafy section of the plant should not be in water. Pull a polythene bag over the coriander and container and refrigerate the whole thing. The fresh coriander should last for weeks. Every other day, pick off and discard the yellowing leaves. If you cannot find fresh coriander, use parsley as a substitute.

Coriander seeds, whole and ground

Dhania, sabut and pisa

These are the round, beige seeds of the coriander plant. They are used a lot in Indian cooking, generally in their ground form. You may buy them, already ground, from supermarkets and Indian and Pakistani grocers. You could also buy the whole seeds and grind them yourself in small quantities in an electric coffee-grinder. I like to put my home-ground coriander seeds through a sieve though this is not essential.

Ground coriander seeds, if stored for several months, begin to taste a little like sawdust. It is best to discard them at this stage and start off with a fresh batch.

Coriander seeds & Ground coriander

Cumin seeds, whole and ground

Zeera, sabut and pisa

These caraway-like seeds are used very frequently in Indian food, both in their whole and ground forms. The whole seeds are sold by Indian and Pakistani grocers and by some supermarkets. The ground seeds can be found in nearly all supermarkets. Whole seeds keep their flavour much longer and may be ground very easily in an electric coffee-grinder.

Roasted cumin seeds

Put 4-5 tablespoons of whole cumin seeds into a small, heavy frying pan (cast-iron frying pans are best for this) and place the pan over a medium flame. No fat is necessary. Stir the seeds and keep roasting them until they turn a few shades darker. Soon you will be able to recognize the wonderful 'roasted' aroma that these seeds emit when they are ready. Store in an airtight container.

Ground roasted cumin seeds

Empty the roasted seeds into an electric coffee-grinder or other spice grinder and grind them finely. You could also use a pestle and mortar for this or else put the seeds between two sheets of brown paper and crush them with a rolling pin. Store ground roasted cumin seeds in a tightly lidded jar.

Cumin seeds, black

Shah zeera or kala zeera

These fine seeds, darker and more expensive than regular cumin seeds, are sold only by Indian and Pakistani grocers. They look like caraway seeds but have a gentle flavour. Buy them whole. If you cannot find them, use regular cumin seeds as a substitute.

Fennel seeds

Sonf

These seeds taste and look like anise seeds only they are larger, plumper and milder. They give meat and vegetables a delicious, liquorice-like flavour. They may be bought from some super-markets and all Indian and Pakistani grocers. Indians often eat roasted fennel seeds after a meal as a digestive and mouth freshener.

Garam masala

This is an aromatic mixture that generally incorporates spices which are supposed to heat the body (the words mean 'hot spices') such as large black cardamoms, cinnamon, black cumin (also called *shah zeera* or royal cumin), cloves, black peppercorns and nutmeg. The mixture is used sparingly and is generally put into foods towards the end of their cooking period. It is also used as a garnish — a final aromatic flavouring sprinkled over cooked meats, vegetables and pulses. It is not a standardized spice mixture. Apart from the fact that there are many regional variations, I am sure that every North Indian and Pakistani home has its own family recipe. The recipe here happens to be one of my favourites. I have substituted seeds from the green cardamom pods for the more traditional black ones as I find their taste to be far more delicate.

Indian and Pakistani grocers and some supermarkets do sell a ready-made garam masala which you may certainly resort to in emergencies. However, you will find it quite pallid, as cheaper spices, such as cumin and coriander, are often substituted for the more expensive cardamom and cloves.

It is best to grind garam masala in small quantities so that it stays fresh. My recipe makes about 3 tablespoons.

1 tablespoon cardamom seeds
5 cm (2 inch) piece of cinnamon stick
1 teaspoon black cumin seeds (use regular cumin seeds as a substitute)
1 teaspoon whole cloves
1 teaspoon black peppercorns
¼ of a nutmeg

Place all the ingredients in a clean, electric coffee-grinder (or any other spice grinder). Turn the machine on for 30-40 seconds or until the spices are finely ground. Store in a small jar with a tight-fitting lid. Keep away from heat and sunlight.

Ground cumin

Cumin seeds

Roasted cumin seeds

Ground roasted cumin

Black cumin seeds

Fennel seeds

Fennel seeds

Cinnamon

Cardamom

Cumin seeds

Cloves

Black peppercorns

Nutmeg

Garam masala

Ground
ginger

Fresh
ginger

Slices of fresh ginger

Kalonji

Ginger, dried ground

Sonth

This is ginger that is dried and powdered, the same that you might use to make gingerbread. It is available in all supermarkets.

Ginger, fresh

Adrak

This light brown, knobbly 'root' is not a root at all but a rhizome with a refreshing, pungent flavour. Its potato-like skin needs to be peeled away before it can be chopped, sliced, grated or made into a paste. To grate ginger into a pulp, use the finest part of a hand grater. To grind ginger into a paste, chop it coarsely first and then throw it into the container of a food processor or blender. Add just enough water to make as smooth a paste as possible.

Fresh ginger, a very common ingredient in Indian cooking, is now sold by many supermarkets. It is certainly sold by all Asian grocers. When buying ginger, look for pieces that are not too wrinkled but have a taut skin. If you use ginger infrequently, 'store' ginger by planting it in a somewhat dry, sandy soil. Water it infrequently. Your ginger will not only survive, but will also sprout fresh knobs. Whenever you need some, dig it up, break off a knob and then plant the rest again. If you use ginger frequently, store it in a cool, airy basket along with your onions, potatoes and garlic.

Kalonji

This spice is a small, black, teardrop-shaped onion seed with an appealing, earthy aroma. It is used for cooking vegetable and fish dishes in Bengal. The rest of the country uses it for pickling. Some north Indian breads such as naans have these seeds sprinkled on them before they are baked. *Kalonji* is sold in Indian and Pakistani stores.

Mustard oil

Sarson ka tel

This yellow oil made from mustard seeds is quite pungent when raw and amazingly sweet when heated to a slight haze. It is used in Bengal and Kashmir for cooking vegetables and fish. It is the favourite oil throughout India for pickling. It is available only at Indian and Pakistani grocers. If you cannot find it, ground nut oil may be substituted.

Mustard seeds, whole black

Sarson

Once you start using these seeds, you will not want to stop. They are round, tiny and not really black but a dark reddish-brown colour. When scattered into hot oil they turn deliciously nutty. If you want to know what they taste like in isolation, make the Gujerati carrot salad (page 123). They are the main seasoning in that dish. Mustard seeds are available at Indian and Pakistani grocers.

Nutmeg

Jaiphal

Buy whole nutmegs. They are sold in many supermarkets, fine delicatessens and all Indian and Pakistani stores. If a recipe calls for a third of a nutmeg, just hit a nutmeg lightly with a hammer. It is very soft and breaks quite easily.

Saffron

Zaafraan or kesar

Saffron threads are the stigma of special crocuses that, in India, grow in the northern state of Kashmir. Saffron *is* expensive. It is used in festive dishes both for its saffron colour and its aroma. Yellow food colouring, or a small pinch of turmeric, may be substituted for the real thing even though purists would disapprove.

To get the most colour and flavour out of saffron, Indians often roast the threads lightly in a heavy cast-iron frying pan and then crumble them into a small amount of hot milk. This milk is then poured into rice and meat dishes as well as desserts.

Saffron is sold in some supermarkets, all

Nutmeg

Black
mustard se

Nutmeg

Saffron

Spice seller,
Udaipur, Rajasthan

Sesame
seeds

Salt

esame
eds

ound
meric

rmeric

fine delicatessens and most Indian and Pakistani groceries. Powdered saffron is also available in selected shops.

Salt

Amounts of salt given in recipes can be adjusted to suit individual tastes.

Sesame seeds

Til

I use the beige, unhulled seeds that are sold in all health food stores and all Oriental grocers. They have a wonderful, nutty flavour, specially after they have been roasted.

Turmeric

Haldi

This is the spice that makes many Indian foods yellow. Apart from its mild, earthy flavour, it is used mainly because it is a digestive and an antiseptic. Fresh turmeric looks like the baby sister of fresh ginger. They are both rhizomes. The only kind of turmeric I have seen in Britain is the dried variety. Buy the ground kind. Use it carefully as it can stain. It is widely available and can be bought at all supermarkets.

Vark

This airy, real silver tissue is used for garnishing sweets as well as festive meat and rice dishes. It is sold only at some Indian and Pakistani grocers. Each silver tissue is packed between sheets of paper. Remove the top sheet carefully. Then pick up the next sheet with the *vark* on it and overturn it gently on the food you wish to garnish. Try not to let the *vark* disintegrate. It *is* edible. Store it in a tightly closed tin as it can tarnish.

Vark

Vegetable oil

Most of my recipes call, rather generally, for vegetable oil. You could use what is labelled as vegetable oil in the supermarkets or you could use groundnut oil, corn oil or sunflower oil. All would be quite suitable.

Yellow and red food colourings

These are used on some Indian foods — for instance these give tandoori food its distinctive colouring. They are vegetable colourings and have no taste. However, one word of warning: a few people (and that includes me!) are allergic to the tartrazine contained in these colourings.

15

Techniques

INDIAN FOOD is unique in its imaginative use of spices, seasonings and flavourings. Many of our cooking techniques are really ways of getting these same spices, seasonings and flavourings to yield as great a variety of tastes and textures as possible. Spices and herbs do not have single, limited tastes. Depending upon the way in which they are used – whole, ground, roasted, fried – they can be coaxed into producing a much larger spectrum than you might first imagine. Herein lies the true genius of Indian cooking.

It amuses me to find that many of the techniques used in the 'Nouvelle Cuisine' of France have been used in India for centuries. We are told that sauces can be made much lighter if they are thickened with ingredients other than flour. Flour is almost never used as a thickener for Indian sauces. Instead, we have used, very cleverly, I might add, ingredients such as onions, garlic, ginger, yogurt and tomatoes.

I think it might be useful, before you actually start cooking a recipe from this book, to measure and prepare all the ingredients you need for the recipe and have them ready near the cooker. Once you are experienced, this will not matter as much. But for those of you who are new to Indian cookery, it will help if you make all your pastes and do all your chopping and measuring before you start. The reason for this is that many Indian dishes require you to cook in one, flowing sweep. Ingredient follows ingredient, often swiftly. Frequently there is no time to stop and hunt for a spice that is hidden in the back of a cupboard. Something on the cooker might burn if you do. So organize yourself and read the recipe carefully. If many of the ingredients go into the saucepan or frying pan at the same time, you can measure them out in advance and keep them in the same bowl or plate, so that they are ready to add without hesitation.

Here are some of the more commonly used techniques in Indian cookery:

Clarified butter

Ghee

Not all Indian food is cooked in ghee, as some people imagine. Many of our foods are *meant* to be cooked in vegetable oil. But ghee does have a rich, nutty taste and a spoonful of it is frequently put on top of cooked pulses to enrich them and give them a silky smoothness. I must add here that there are certain families in India (not ours) who have always cooked in ghee. There used to be a certain amount of status attached to being able to say, 'We use nothing but pure ghee.' But today, even these families are coming around to using unsaturated fats.

I feel that cooking in ghee is a bit like cooking in butter. It is fine to do it some of the time for certain selected dishes. Some of my recipes do call for ghee. I suggest you buy it, ready-made, from Asian grocers. However, if you wish to make it yourself, melt 450g (1 lb) unsalted butter in a small heavy pan over a low flame. Then let it simmer very gently for 10-30 minutes. The length of the time will depend upon the amount of water in the butter. As soon as the white, milky residue turns to golden particles (you have to keep watching), strain the ghee through several layers of cheesecloth. Cool, then pour into a clean jar. Cover. Properly made ghee does not need refrigeration.

Dropping spices into hot oil

Baghaar

I do not know of this technique being used anywhere else in the world. Oil (or ghee) is heated until it is extremely hot, but not burning. Then spices, generally whole ones, or else chopped up garlic and ginger, are added to the oil. The seasonings immediately begin to swell, brown, pop, or otherwise change character. This seasoned oil, together with all the spices in it, is then poured over cooked foods such as pulses and vegetables or else uncooked foods are added to it and then sautéed or simmered.

16

The seasonings that are most commonly used for *baghaar* include whole cumin seeds, whole black mustard seeds, whole fennel seeds, dried red chillies, cloves, cinnamon sticks, cardamom pods, bay leaves, black peppercorns, as well as chopped up garlic and ginger. Hot oil transforms them all and gives them a new, more concentrated character. When the whole spices used are large, such as bay leaves, cinnamon sticks or even cloves and peppercorns, they are not meant to be eaten but are left to one side of the plate along with any bones.

Using a grinding stone, Vadala, Maharashtra, Central India

Grinding spices

Many recipes call for ground spices. In India, we generally buy our spices whole and then grind them ourselves as we need them. They have much more flavour this way. You probably already know the difference between freshly ground black pepper and ground pepper that has been sitting around for a month. The same applies to all spices. In India, the grinding of spices is generally done on heavy grinding stones. We, in our modern kitchens, can get the same results without the labour by using an electric coffee-grinder. It is best to grind limited quantities so that the spices do not lose their flavour. If you wipe the grinder carefully after use there will be no 'aftertaste' of spices to flavour your coffee beans.

Buying ground spices is perfectly all right as long as you know that they will be less potent as time goes on. Before buying your spices, consult the preceding chapter to see which spices you must buy whole and which you may buy ground.

Roasting spices

This brings out yet another flavour from the spices. In my home, for example, we always make yogurt relishes with cumin that has been roasted first and then ground. Nothing else will do. Ordinary ground cumin has a different flavour, quite unsuitable for putting into foods that are not going to be cooked. This roasting is best done in a heavy, cast iron frying pan since the pan can be heated without putting oil or water into it first. Whole spices are put into the pan. The pan is then shaken around until the spices turn a shade or two darker and emit their new 'roasted' aroma. You will begin to recognise it after you have done it a few times.

Making thick sauces

Many of our meat, poultry and fish dishes have thick, dark sauces. My mother always said that the mark of a good chef was his sauce which depended not only on a correct balance of all the ingredients, but the correct frying (*bhuno*-ing) of these ingredients.

As I stated earlier, there is no flour in these sauces. The 'body' comes, very often, from onions, garlic and ginger. The rich brown colour comes from frying all these ingredients properly. Very often, we make a paste of one or more of these ingredients first. In India, this has been done for centuries on a grinding stone but in western kitchens it can be done easily in food processors and blenders, sometimes with the aid of a little water.

Once the paste has been made, it needs to be browned or the sauce will not have the correct flavour and colour. This is best done in a heavy pan, preferably a non-stick one, in a

17

generous amount of oil. Remember that extra oil can always be spooned off the top once the dish has been cooked.

Browning sliced or chopped onions and garlic

Sometimes a recipe requires that you brown thinly sliced or chopped onions. I have noticed that many of the students in my cookery classes stop half-way and when I point out to them that the onions are not quite done, they say 'Oh, but if we cook them more, they will burn.' They will not, not if you watch. Start the frying on a medium-high flame and turn the heat down somewhat as the onions lose their water and begin to turn brown. They do need to be a rich reddish-brown colour or your sauce — if that is what they are intended for — will be pale and weak.

The same goes for garlic. There is a common misconception that if garlic is allowed to pick up any colour at all, it will turn bitter. Actually, garlic tastes quite superb if it is chopped and allowed to fry in oil until it turns a medium-brown colour. I often cook courgettes this way — in oil that has been flavoured with browned garlic. Spinach and cauliflower tastes good this way too. In India, we say that such dishes are cooked with a garlic *baghaar*. A garlic *baghaar* can, of course, just be the first step in a recipe. More spices would be added later.

Adding yogurt to sauces

Yogurt adds a creamy texture and a delicate tartness to many of our sauces. But yogurt curdles when it is heated. So when we add it to our browning sauces, we add just a tablespoon at a time. After 1 tablespoon of yogurt has been put in, it is stirred and fried until it is absorbed and 'accepted' by the sauce. Then the next tablespoon is added.

Peeling and chopping tomatoes

Many of my recipes call for peeled and chopped tomatoes. To peel them, bring a saucepan of water to a rolling boil. Drop in the tomatoes and leave them for 15 seconds. Drain, rinse the tomatoes under cold water and peel them. Now chop the tomatoes, making sure that you save all the juice that comes out of them. In India, we very rarely seed tomatoes. Many people do not even bother to peel them, though I do feel that this improves the texture of a sauce.

Reducing sauces

Sometimes meat is allowed to cook in a fairly thin, brothy sauce. Then the lid of the saucepan is removed and the sauce reduced over a fairly high flame until it is thick and clings to the meat. The meat has to be stirred frequently at this stage, so that it does not catch and burn.

Cooking chicken without its skin

In India, we almost always remove the skin of the chicken before we cook it. The flavour of the spices penetrates the chicken much better this way and the entire dish is less fatty. It is very easy to remove the skin. Just hold it with a paper towel so that it does not slip, and pull!

Marinating

We often cut deep gashes in large pieces of meat and leave them overnight in a marinade of yogurt and seasonings. The yogurt tenderizes the meat while the gashes allow the flavour to penetrate deep inside the meat. After this, the meat can be grilled or baked faster than usual.

Browning meats

In India, we generally do not brown cubes of meat by themselves but brown them with the sauce instead. I find this hard to do with British meats because they release far too much water as they cook. Indian meats tend to be very fresh and have far less water in them. So to avoid this problem I brown my meat a few pieces at a time in hot oil and set them aside. Once I have made the sauce, I add the browned meat cubes (and all the good juices that come out of them) and let them cook.

These are just a few of the techniques that we use in Indian cookery. Others, that have to do with cooking rice and pulses, I shall deal with later in the appropriate chapters.

EQUIPMENT

IF YOU ARE going to cook authentic Indian food, do you need any special equipment?

For those of you who already have a well equipped kitchen, the answer is probably 'no'. Good knives, sturdy pans with a good distribution of heat, rolling pins, graters, bowls, slotted spoons, pestle and mortar, frying pans — I am sure you have these already.

There are, however, a few items that make the cooking of Indian food simpler.

Food processor or blender

Every Indian home has a grinding stone. This consists of a large flat stone that just sits and a smaller one that is moved manually on top of it and does the actual grinding. These stones are exceedingly heavy. It is just as well that they are no longer essential. Their place, in modern kitchens, can be taken by food processors and blenders. Onions, garlic and ginger, formerly ground on grinding stones, can now be made into a paste in electrically powered machines.

If you do not have a food processor or blender, then there are ways around it. Garlic, for example, may be mashed in a mortar or put through a garlic press. Ginger may be grated on the finest part of the grater. Onions can just be chopped very finely. Sometimes my recipe suggests putting water into the food processor while making the paste. If you have crushed the garlic and grated the ginger by hand, just put them into a bowl and add the amount of water in the recipe.

Electric coffee grinder

Food processors and blenders cannot do all the work of an Indian grinding stone. Dry spices, for example, cannot be ground in them properly. For this, only a coffee-grinder will do. A coffee-grinder grinds spices in seconds and can then be wiped clean. If you do not have one, you will have to crush your spices in small quantities with a pestle and mortar.

Large non-stick frying pan with a lid

Non-stick pans take the worry out of cooking many foods. Browning meats do not stick to the bottom, nor do sauces with ginger or almonds. As metal spoons ruin the finish of non-stick utensils, use plastic or wooden ones.

Cast-iron frying pans

I keep a 13 cm (5 inch) cast-iron frying pan for roasting spices — it can heat without oil or water in it — and for doing *baghaar*, frying small amounts of spices in oil. A larger cast-iron pan is excellent for making Indian breads such as *parathas* and *chapatis*. In India, these breads are cooked on a *tava*, a round, concave cast-iron plate. A large cast-iron frying pan makes the best substitute.

Karhai

This is very similar to a Chinese wok. If you took a large, hollow ball and cut it into half, that would be about the shape of a karhai. I am not suggesting that you go out and buy a karhai. I just wish to point out that for deep-frying, it is perhaps the most economical utensil as it allows you to use a relatively small quantity of oil while giving you enough depth in the centre of the utensil to submerge foods. A deep frying pan can be used instead.

Electric rice cooker

If you frequently cook large quantities of rice, an electric rice cooker can be a useful piece of equipment. The cooker has a large covered pan which sits on top of an electric element. When the water has been absorbed by the rice, the cooker switches itself off, and will then keep the rice warm for several hours. The preparation of the rice and the amount of water you use to cook it in are identical to the conventional methods of cooking rice (page 103).

Menus

WHAT DO YOU eat with what? With each recipe in this book, I have suggested a menu. You do not have to follow it. After all, the fun of eating is to follow your own palate and put together dishes that are convenient and exciting for you.

Generally speaking, an Indian meal consists of a meat dish, a vegetable dish, bread and or rice, a pulse dish, a yogurt relish (or plain yogurt) and a fresh chutney or small, relish-like salad. Pickles and preserved chutneys may be added if you have them. Fruits, rather than desserts, are served at the end of a meal, although on festive occasions, sweets would not be at all amiss. Sometimes, when the meat dish is particularly elegant and rich, we eliminate the pulse and serve an equally elegant *pullao* rice. Vegetarians — and there are millions in India — increase the number of vegetable and pulse dishes and always serve yogurt in some form.

Within this general framework, we try to see that the dishes we serve vary in colour, texture and flavour. If the meat has a lot of sauce, then we often serve a 'dry', unsauced vegetable with it. If the vegetable we are serving is very soft — such as spinach — we make sure that there is a crunchy relish on the table.

Most Indians like to eat with their hands. The more Westernised ones may use knives and forks or spoons and forks, or just forks, but they too succumb every now and then to the pleasure of eating with their fingers.

It is only the right hand that is used for eating, the left being considered 'unclean'. With it, we break pieces of bread and then use the pieces to scoop up some meat or vegetable. With it, we also form neat morsels out of rice and other accompanying dishes and then transport them to our mouths. In the northern states such as Uttar Pradesh, this is done very delicately with just the tips of the fingers. In the south, almost the entire hand may be used.

When we serve ourselves, we put most foods beside each other on our plates. Only very wet, flowing dishes are sometimes ladled on top of the rice but not on top of *all* the rice. Some of the rice is left plain to enable us to eat

it with other dishes. Very wet dishes that are meant to be eaten with bread are served in small, individual bowls.

This is all very well if you are cooking a whole Indian meal. If you feel like making such a meal, then by all means do it. On the other hand, there is no reason why you cannot serve an Indian vegetable with your roast lamb or eat an Indian meat with French bread and salad.

Here is a selection of Indian menus. The first menu is illustrated on the title page and another is illustrated opposite.

Prawns in a sauce, *Rasedar jhinga* (page 68)
Plain basmati rice, *Basmati chaaval* (page 107)
Cauliflower with potatoes, *Phool gobi aur aloo ki bhaji* (page 83)
Tomato, onion and green coriander relish, *Cachumber* (page 124)

Mughlai lamb with turnips, *Shabdeg* (page 37)
Mushroom pullao, *Khumbi pullao* (page 110)
Spicy green beans, *Masaledar sem* (page 78)
Yogurt with cucumber and mint, *Kheere ka raita* (page 119)

Black-eyed beans with mushrooms, *Lobhia aur khumbi* (page 94)
Cauliflower with onion and tomato, *Phool gobi ki bhaji* (page 82)
Layered bread, *Paratha* (page 98)
Gujerati carrot salad, *Gajar ka salad* (page 123)

Sweet yellow rice, *Meetha pullao* (page 112)
Gujerati-style green beans, *Gujerati sem* (page 78)
Whole leg of lamb in a spicy yogurt sauce, *Raan masaledar* (page 38)

Beef baked with yogurt and black pepper, *Dum gosht* (page 27)
The Lake Palace Hotel's aubergine cooked in the pickling style, *Baigan achari* (page 77)
Rice with peas, *Tahiri* (page 109)
Tomato, onion and green coriander relish, *Cachumber* (page 124)

Clockwise from top left: Sweet and sour
okra (page 87); Gujerati carrot salad
(page 123); Lamb and rice casserole
(Mughlai biryani, page 114)

Street scene, Udaipur, Rajasthan

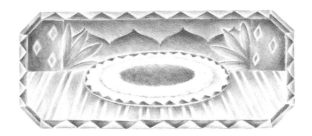

MEAT

THIS CHAPTER has a great variety of meat dishes in it, going from *Kheema matar* (Minced meat with peas) and *Chhole wala gosht* (Pork chops with chickpeas) that you may wish to cook for your family, to *Raan masaledar* (Whole leg of lamb in a spicy yogurt sauce garnished with almonds and raisins) — which would impress the most blasé of guests.

There are a lot of lamb recipes. We do eat a fair amount of lamb in India. I love English lamb. I realise that it is a bit expensive but it does have excellent flavour.

I find the best cuts of lamb for stewing come from the neck and shoulder. Butchers try to sell leg of lamb for stewing, mainly because it is easier to cut up. If you can, insist upon shoulder. There is a lot of connective tissue in the shoulder and neck. This makes for a moister meat.

In India, we usually leave the bone in the meat when we are cooking any stew-type dish. In fact, we throw in a few extra marrow bones for good measure because they affect the taste and texture of the sauce.

Many recipes in this book call for boned lamb. This is only because, over the years, I have seen many guests struggle with bones and have come to the conclusion that just because I like bones (I suck them), there is no reason to inflict them upon my guests. A majority of people who dine in our house seem to prefer boned meat. I leave the bone-in or bone-out decision up to you. Just remember that bones in stewing meat such as shoulder make up about 40 per cent of the total volume.

In India, we frequently cook meat with vegetables such as potatoes and turnips. The vegetables absorb the taste of the meat and lend their own flavour to the sauce.

I have included a few recipes for beef and pork as there are many communities in India which eat them. I, for one, simply love the *Dum gosht* (Beef baked with yogurt and black pepper) as well as the *Vindaloo* (Goan-style hot and sour pork), from India's west coast.

23

Minced lamb with mint

Pudine wala kheema

THIS DISH, with its refreshing minty flavour, may be served very simply with rice, a pulse, such as Whole green lentils with spinach and ginger (page 91) and a yogurt relish.
I often use it to stuff tomatoes in the summer. If you wish to do this, get firm, good-sized tomatoes and slice off a cap at the top. Scoop out the inside without breaking the skin and then season the inside of the tomato generously with salt and pepper. Stuff it loosely with the mince, put the caps back on and bake the tomatoes in a moderately hot oven (200°C, 400°F, Gas Mark 6) for about 15 minutes or until the skin begins to crinkle. Serve with rice and salad.

PREPARATION TIME: 20 minutes   COOKING TIME: 45 minutes

Serves 6
175 g (6 oz) onions, peeled
8-9 garlic cloves, peeled
1 × 5 × 2.5 cm (2 × 1 inch) piece of fresh ginger, peeled and coarsely chopped
3 tablespoons water
2 tablespoons ground cumin
4 teaspoons ground coriander
1 teaspoon ground turmeric
1/4-1 teaspoon cayenne pepper
4 tablespoons vegetable oil
4 cardamom pods
6 cloves
1 kg (2 lb) minced lamb
about 1 1/2 teaspoons salt
50 g (2 oz) finely chopped fresh mint leaves
1/4 teaspoon garam masala (page 13)
1 1/2 tablespoons lemon juice

1.   Chop half the onions finely and set them aside. Chop the other half coarsely and put them, along with the garlic, ginger and the water into the container of an electric blender. Blend until you have a smooth paste. Empty the paste into a small bowl. Add the cumin, coriander, turmeric and cayenne. Mix.
2.   Heat the oil in a 25 cm (10 inch) frying pan over a high flame. When it is hot, put in the cardamom and cloves. Two seconds later, put in the finely chopped onions. Stir and fry them until they turn fairly brown. Turn the heat to medium and put in the spice mixture from the small bowl. Stir and fry for 3-4 minutes. If the spice mixture sticks to the pan, sprinkle in 1 tablespoon of water and keep frying.
3.   Put in the minced meat. Break up all the lumps and stir the mince about until it loses all its pinkness. Stir and fry another minute after that. Add the salt and mix. Cover, turn the heat to very low and let the mince cook in its own juices for 25 minutes. Remove the lid and spoon off most of the accumulated fat. Add the chopped mint, garam masala and lemon juice. Stir to mix and bring to a simmer. Cover, and simmer on a very low heat for 3 minutes.
4.   The whole cardamoms and cloves in this dish are not meant to be eaten.

Minced meat with peas

Kheema matar

I ASSOCIATE THIS DISH with very pleasurable family picnics which we had, sometimes in the private compartments of slightly sooty, steam-engined trains, and sometimes in the immaculate public gardens of historic Moghul palaces. The mince, invariably at room temperature, was eaten with pooris or parathas that had been stacked tightly in aluminium containers. There was always a pickle to perk things up and an onion relish as well.
Serve with rice and a salad.

PREPARATION TIME: 15 minutes
COOKING TIME: about 1 hour

Clockwise from the left: Minced lamb with mint and Plain basmati rice (page 107); Minced meat with peas;
Fresh coriander chutney (page 121); Onion relish (page 125)

Serves 4-6

4 tablespoons vegetable oil
75 g (3 oz) onion, peeled and finely chopped
6-7 medium garlic cloves, peeled and finely chopped
750 g (1½ lb) minced lamb (or use minced beef)
1×2.5 cm (1 inch) cube of fresh ginger, peeled and grated to a pulp
1-2 fresh hot green chillies, minced
1 teaspoon ground coriander
1 teaspoon ground cumin
⅛-¼ teaspoon cayenne pepper
300 ml (½ pint) water
175-200 g (6-7 oz) shelled peas
6 tablespoons chopped fresh coriander
about 1¼ teaspoons salt
1 teaspoon garam masala (page 13)
about 1½ tablespoons lemon juice

1. Heat the oil in a wide, medium saucepan over a medium-high flame. When it is hot, put in the onions. Stir and fry them until they are lightly browned. Add the garlic. Stir and fry for another minute. Now put in the mince, ginger, green chillies, coriander, cumin and cayenne. Stir and fry the meat for 5 minutes, breaking up any lumps as you do so. Add 175 ml (6 fl oz) of the water and bring to a boil. Cover, turn the heat to low, and simmer gently for 30 minutes.

2. Add the peas, fresh coriander, salt, garam masala, lemon juice and the remaining water. Mix and bring to a simmer. Cover and cook on a low heat for another 10 minutes or until the peas are tender. Taste for seasoning and adjust the balance of salt and lemon juice if you need to.

3. A lot of fat might collect at the bottom of your pan. When you get ready to serve, lift the mince and peas out of the fat with a slotted spoon. Do not serve the fat.

Kashmiri meatballs

Kashmiri koftas

THESE SAUSAGE-SHAPED MEATBALLS taste very Kashmiri in their blend of flavours. I often serve them with Plain basmati rice (page 107), Red split lentils with cumin seed (page 90), and Carrot and onion salad (page 123).

PREPARATION TIME: 25 minutes
COOKING TIME: about 45 minutes–1 hour

Serves 6
1 kg (2 lb) minced lamb
1 × 4 × 2.5 cm (1½ × 1 inch) piece of fresh ginger, peeled and finely grated
1 tablespoon ground cumin
1 tablespoon ground coriander
¼ teaspoon ground cloves
¼ teaspoon ground cinnamon
⅛ teaspoon grated nutmeg
¼ teaspoon freshly ground black pepper
⅛-¼ teaspoon cayenne pepper
about 1¼ teaspoons salt
5 tablespoons plain yogurt
7-8 tablespoons vegetable oil
5 cm (2 inch) piece of cinnamon stick
5-6 cardamom pods
2 bay leaves
5-6 cloves
8 fl oz (250 ml) warm water

1. Combine the lamb, ginger, cumin, coriander, ground cloves, ground cinnamon, grated nutmeg, black pepper, cayenne, salt and 3 tablespoons of the yogurt in a bowl. Mix well.
2. Wet your hands with cold water and form 24 long koftas – sausage shapes, about 6-7.5 cm (2½-3 inches) long and about 2.5 cm (1 inch) thick.
3. Heat the oil in a large, preferably non-stick, frying pan. When it is hot, put in the cinnamon, cardamom, bay leaves and whole cloves. Stir for a second. Now put in the koftas

From the top: Kashmiri meatballs with Plain basmati rice (page 107) and Carrot and onion salad (page 123); Beef baked with yogurt and black pepper; Chapati (page 100)

in a single layer and fry on a medium-high heat until they are lightly browned on all sides.

4.   Beat the remaining yogurt into the warm water. Pour this over the koftas and bring to a boil. Cover, lower the heat and simmer for about 30 minutes, turning the koftas around gently every 7-8 minutes. By then no liquid other than the fat should be left. If necessary, turn up the heat to achieve this.

5.   When you get ready to serve, lift the koftas out of the fat with a slotted spoon. Leave the whole spices behind as well.

Beef baked with yogurt and black pepper

Dum gosht

EVER SINCE the Moghuls came to India, there has been a method of cooking that Indians refer to as *dum*. Meat (or rice) is partially cooked in a heavy pot and then covered over with a flat lid. At this stage the pot and lid are sealed with a 'rope' made out of very stiff dough. The pot is placed over a gentle fire – generally the last of the charcoals – and more hot charcoals are spread over the lid. The meat proceeds to cook very slowly until it is tender, often in small amounts of liquid. In today's world, this *dum* method of cooking is the equivalent of slow oven baking. So what I have done here is to update a very traditional, top-of-the-cooker, Moghul recipe. As with many other *dum* foods, this is not a dish with a lot of sauce. Ideally, whatever sauce there is should be thick and cling to the meat. If you like, you could leave out the cayenne in this recipe. That is probably what the early Moghuls did. The later Moghuls, seduced by the chilli peppers brought over from the New World by the Portuguese, used it generously.

I love to eat this meat dish with chapatis or parathas or naans. If you prefer rice, then the more moist pullaos, such as Mushroom pullao (page 110), would be the perfect accompaniment. You could also make this dish with stewing lamb meat from the shoulder.

PREPARATION TIME: 20 minutes
COOKING TIME: about 2¼ hours   OVEN: 180°C, 350°F, Gas Mark 4

Serves 4-6

6 tablespoons vegetable oil

1 kg (2 lb) boneless stewing beef from the neck and shoulder, cut into 4 cm (1½ inch) cubes

225 g (8 oz) onions, peeled and very finely chopped

6 garlic cloves, peeled and very finely chopped

½ teaspoon ground ginger

⅛-½ teaspoon cayenne pepper

1 tablespoon paprika

2 teaspoons salt

½ teaspoon very coarsely ground black pepper

300 ml (½ pint) plain yogurt, beaten lightly

1.   Heat the oil in a wide flameproof casserole over a medium-high flame. When it is hot, put in as many pieces of meat as the casserole will hold easily in a single layer. Brown the meat pieces all over and set them aside in a bowl. Brown all the meat this way.

2.   Put the onions and garlic into the same pan and turn down the heat to medium. Stir and fry the onion-garlic mixture for about 10 minutes or until it has browned. Now put in the browned meat as well as any juices that might have accumulated in the bowl. Add the ginger, cayenne, paprika, salt and pepper. Stir for 1 minute.

3.   Now put in the yogurt and bring to a simmer. Cover tightly, first with aluminium foil and then with a lid, and bake in a preheated oven for 1½ hours. The meat should be tender by now. If it is not, pour in about 150 ml (¼ pint) of boiling water, cover tightly and bake another 20-30 minutes. Stir the meat gently before serving.

Lamb with onions

Do piaza

THIS IS AN ELEGANT DISH that may be made as mild or as hot as you like. It is cooked with a fair amount of oil but most of this is skimmed off the top before serving. There are some whole spices in it — cloves, cardamom and cinnamon — which are not meant to be eaten. They should be pushed to the side as and when you come across them on your plates.
Lamb with onions may be served with rice or a bread. Spicy green beans (page 78) also go well.

PREPARATION TIME: 35 minutes   COOKING TIME: 1¼ hours

Serves 6

4 good-sized onions, peeled
7 garlic cloves, peeled
1 × 2.5 cm (1 inch) cube of fresh ginger, coarsely chopped
450 ml (¾ pint) water
10 tablespoons vegetable oil
2.5 cm (1 inch) piece of cinnamon stick
10 cardamom pods
10 cloves
1.25 kg (2½ lb) boned lamb, preferably from the shoulder, cut into 2.5 cm (1 inch) cubes (fat removed)
1 tablespoon ground coriander
2 teaspoons ground cumin
6 tablespoons plain yogurt, lightly beaten
¼-½ teaspoon cayenne pepper
about 1¼ teaspoons salt
½ teaspoon garam masala (page 13)

1.   Slice 3 of the onions into halves lengthwise and then cut them, crosswise, into very fine half rings. Chop the remaining onion finely. Keep the 2 types of onion separate.
2.   Put the garlic and ginger into the container of an electric blender or food processor. Add 120 ml (4 fl oz) of the water and blend until fairly smooth.
3.   Heat the oil in a wide, heavy saucepan over a medium-high flame. When it is hot, put in the finely sliced onions. Stir and fry for 10-12 minutes or until the onions turn a nice, reddish-brown colour. You may have to turn the heat down somewhat towards the end of this cooking period. Remove the onions with a slotted spoon and spread them on a plate lined with paper towels.
4.   Put the cinnamon, cardamom and cloves into the hot oil. Stir them about for about 5 seconds over a medium-high heat. Now put in 8-10 cubes of meat or as many as the saucepan will hold easily in a single, loosely packed layer. Brown the meat on one side. turn it over and brown the other side. Remove the meat cubes with a slotted spoon and put them in a bowl. Brown all the meat this way, removing each batch as it is done.
5.   Put the chopped onion into the remaining oil in the saucepan. Stir and fry it on a medium heat until the pieces turn brown at the edges. Add the garlic-ginger paste. Stir and fry it until all the water in it seems to boil away and you see the oil again. Turn the heat down a bit and add the coriander and cumin. Stir and fry for 30 seconds. Now add 1 tablespoon of the yogurt. Stir and fry until it is incorporated into the sauce. Add another tablespoon of yogurt. Stir and fry, incorporating this into the sauce as well. Add all the yogurt this way, 1 tablespoon at a time. Now put in all the meat and any accumulated juices in the meat bowl with the remaining water, the cayenne and the salt. Stir to mix and bring to a simmer. Cover, turn the heat to low and cook for about 45 minutes or until the lamb is tender. Add the fried onions and the garam masala. Stir to mix. Cook, uncovered, for another 2-3 minutes, stirring gently as you do so.
6.   Turn off the heat and let the pan sit for a while. The fat will rise to the top. Remove it with a spoon.
7.   The whole spices in this dish are not meant to be eaten.

Clockwise from the left: Red lamb or beef stew (page 30);
Spicy green beans (page 78); Naan (page 99);
Lamb with onions and Plain basmati rice (page 107)

Red lamb or beef stew

Pictured on
page 29

Rogan josh

ROGAN JOSH gets its name from its rich, red appearance. The red appearance, in turn, is derived from ground red chillies, which are used quite generously in this recipe. If you want your dish to have the right colour and not be very hot, combine paprika with cayenne pepper in any proportion that you like. Just make sure that your paprika is fresh and has a good red colour. There are many recipes for *rogan josh*. This is probably the simplest of them all. It may be served with an Indian bread or rice. A green bean or aubergine dish would be a perfect accompaniment.

PREPARATION TIME: 25 minutes
COOKING TIME: 1½ hours for lamb; 2½ hours for beef
OVEN: 180°C, 350°F, Gas Mark 4

Serves 4-6

2 × 2.5 cm (1 inch) cubes of fresh ginger, peeled and coarsely chopped

8 garlic cloves, peeled

4 tablespoons water, plus 300-450 ml (½-¾ pint)

10 tablespoons vegetable oil

1 kg (2 lb) boned meat from lamb shoulder or leg, or stewing beef (chuck), cut into 2.5 cm (1 inch) cubes

10 cardamom pods

2 bay leaves

6 cloves

10 black peppercorns

2.5 cm (1 inch) piece of cinnamon stick

200 g (7 oz) onions, peeled and chopped

1 teaspoon ground coriander

2 teaspoons ground cumin

4 teaspoons bright red paprika mixed with ½-1 teaspoon cayenne pepper

1¼ teaspoons salt

6 tablespoons plain yogurt

¼ teaspoon garam masala (page 13)

freshly ground black pepper

1.   Put the ginger, garlic and 4 tablespoons of water into the container of an electric blender. Blend well until you have a smooth paste.
2.   Heat the oil in a wide, heavy flameproof casserole over a medium-high flame. Brown the meat cubes in several batches and set them to one side. Put the cardamom, bay leaves, cloves, peppercorns and cinnamon into the same hot oil. Stir once and wait until the cloves swell and the bay leaves begin to take on colour. This just takes a few seconds.
3.   Now put in the onions. Stir and fry for about 5 minutes or until the onions turn a medium-brown colour. Put in the ginger-garlic paste and stir for 30 seconds, then the coriander, cumin, paprika-cayenne and salt. Stir and fry for another 30 seconds. Add the fried meat cubes and juices. Stir for 30 seconds.
4.   Now put in 1 tablespoon of the yogurt. Stir and fry for about 30 seconds or until the yogurt is well blended. Add the remaining yogurt, 1 tablespoon at a time, in the same way. Stir and fry for another 3-4 minutes.
5.   Now add 300 ml (½ pint) of water if you are cooking lamb and 450 ml (¾ pint) water if you are cooking beef. Bring the contents of the pan to a boil, scraping in all the browned spices on the sides and bottom of the pan. Cover, turn the heat to low and simmer for about 1 hour for lamb and 2 hours for beef, or until the meat is tender. (The meat could also be baked, covered, in a preheated oven for the same length of time.) Every 10 minutes or so, give the meat a good stir.
6.   When the meat is tender, take off the lid, turn the heat up to medium, and boil away some of the liquid. You should end up with tender meat in a thick, reddish-brown sauce. All the fat that collects in the pan may be spooned off the top. Sprinkle the garam masala and black pepper over the meat before you serve and mix them in.

Kashmiri red lamb stew

Kashmiri rogan josh

KASHMIRI HINDUS do not eat any onions or garlic and they often use dry, powdered ginger instead of the fresh kind. This is their very different and quite delicious version of *rogan josh*. (For more on *rogan josh*, see the introduction to the preceding recipe.) I have left the bones in the meat this time as most Indians really prefer their meat this way. *Kashmiri rogan josh* may be served with Frozen spinach with potatoes (page 85), Plain long-grain rice (page 107) and a relish.

PREPARATION TIME: 15 minutes
COOKING TIME: 1½ hours

Serves 4-6

1 tablespoon fennel seeds

750 ml (1¼ pints) plain yogurt

6 tablespoons vegetable oil

2 cm (¾ inch) piece of cinnamon stick

6 cloves

pinch of ground asafetida (optional)

1.5 kg (3 lb) shoulder or neck of lamb
(total weight with bone),
cut into 5 cm (2 inch) cubes

2½ teaspoons salt – or to taste

4 teaspoons bright red paprika mixed with
¼-1 teaspoon cayenne pepper

1½ teaspoons ground ginger

900 ml (1½ pints) water

¼ teaspoon garam masala (page 13)

Clockwise from the top: Kashmiri red lamb stew;
Plain long-grain rice (page 107); Tomato, onion
and green coriander relish (page 124)

1. Put the fennel seeds into the container of a spice grinder and grind until fine.
2. Put the yogurt in a bowl and beat it with a fork or a whisk until it is smooth and creamy.
3. Heat the oil in a large saucepan over a high flame. When it is hot, put in the cinnamon and cloves. One second later, put in the ground asafetida, if using. One second after that, put in all the meat and the salt. Stir the meat and cook, still on a high flame, for about 5 minutes. Now put in the paprika and cayenne and give the meat a good stir.
4. Slowly add the yogurt, about 150 ml (¼ pint) at a time, stirring the meat vigorously as you do so. Add all the yogurt this way. Keep cooking on a high heat until all the liquid has boiled away and the meat pieces have browned slightly. Add the fennel and ginger. Give the meat some more good stirs.
5. Now put in the water, cover, leaving the lid very slightly open, and cook on a medium heat for 30 minutes.
6. Cover and cook on a low heat for another 45 minutes or until the meat is tender. Stir a few times as the meat cooks, making sure there is always some liquid in the pan.
7. Remove the lid and add the garam masala. You should have a thick reddish brown sauce. If it is too thin, boil it down a little.

Lamb with spinach

Dilli ka saag gosht

THIS DISH could also be made with beef. Use cubed chuck steak and cook it for about 2 hours or until it is tender. *Dilli ka saag gosht* may be served with rice or bread. I think Fried aubergines slices (page 76) and a yogurt dish would complement the meat well.

PREPARATION TIME: 30 minutes   COOKING TIME: 1½ hours

Serves 6

8 tablespoons vegetable oil

¼ teaspoon whole black peppercorns

6 cloves

2 bay leaves

6 cardamom pods

175 g (6 oz) onions, peeled and finely chopped

6-8 garlic cloves, peeled and finely chopped

1 × 2.5 cm (1 inch) cube of ginger, peeled and finely chopped

1 kg (2 lb) boned meat from a shoulder of lamb, cut into 2.5 cm (1 inch) cubes

2 teaspoons ground cumin

1 teaspoon ground coriander

¼-¾ teaspoon cayenne pepper

salt

5 tablespoons plain yogurt, well beaten

1 kg (2 lb) fresh spinach, trimmed, washed and finely chopped

¼ teaspoon garam masala (page 13)

1.   Heat the oil in a large saucepan over a medium-high flame. When it is hot, put in the peppercorns, cloves, bay leaves and cardamom pods. Stir for 1 second. Now put in the onions, garlic and ginger. Stir and fry until the onions develop brown specks.

2.   Now add the meat, cumin, coriander, cayenne pepper and 1 teaspoon of salt. Stir and fry for 1 minute. Add 1 tablespoon of the beaten yogurt. Stir and fry for another minute. Add another 1 tablespoon of the yogurt. Stir and fry for 1 minute. Keep on doing this until all the yogurt has been incorporated. The meat should also have a slightly browned look. Add the spinach and 1 teaspoon of salt. Stir to mix. Keep stirring and cooking until the spinach wilts completely.

3.   Cover tightly, and simmer on a low heat for about 1¼ hours or until the meat is tender.

4.   Remove the lid and add the garam masala. Turn the heat to medium. Stir and cook for another 5 minutes or until most (but not all) the water in the spinach disappears and you have a thick green sauce.

5.   The whole spices in this dish are not meant to be eaten.

From the left: Lamb with spinach; Paratha (page 98); Kashmiri lamb stew and Plain long-grain rice (page 107)

Kashmiri lamb stew

Kashmiri yakhni

SOME KASHMIRI DISHES are fiercely hot, others mild and soothing. Often, they are served together at the same meal. For those of you who are unused to very spicy foods, this might be the perfect dish to try first. It is really a lamb stew — with lots of lovely fennel flavour but no hot chillies — that is eventually thickened with yogurt so it has a creamy tartness. You could serve it with plain rice, as Kashmiris do.

PREPARATION TIME: 15 minutes   COOKING TIME: 2 hours

Serves 4-6
4 teaspoons fennel seeds
6 tablespoons vegetable oil or ghee
pinch of ground asafetida (optional)
1.5 kg (3 lb) shoulder of lamb, boned or unboned, cut into 5 cm (2 inch) cubes
2.5 cm (1 inch) piece of cinnamon stick
10 cardamom pods
15 cloves
1 ¾ teaspoons salt — or to taste

600 ml (1 pint) water
1 ½ teaspoons ground ginger
450 ml (¾ pint) plain yogurt
¼ teaspoon garam masala (page 13)

1.   Put the fennel seeds into a clean coffee grinder and grind until you have a powder.

2.   Heat the oil in a heavy, wide saucepan over a high heat. When it is hot, put in the asafetida, if using. One second later, put in all the meat, as well as the cinnamon, cardamom, cloves and salt. Stir and cook, uncovered, over a high heat for about 5 minutes or until almost all the water released by the meat disappears and the meat browns very lightly. Lower the heat to medium and add 1 tablespoon water, the fennel and ginger. Stir to mix. Add the measured water, cover partially, and simmer on a medium heat for 30 minutes. Cover completely, turn the heat to low and simmer for 40 minutes or until the meat is tender. Stir a few times as the meat cooks, adding a few tablespoons of water if it seems to dry out.

3.   Beat the yogurt in a bowl until it is smooth and creamy.

4.   Remove the cover and turn the heat to medium-low. Push the meat cubes to the edges of the pan, leaving a space in the centre. Pour the yogurt very slowly into this well, while moving a slotted spoon back and forth quite fast in the same area. (If you do not do this, the yogurt will curdle.) Keep up this movement for a good 5 minutes *after* all the yogurt has been poured in. You should now have a creamy sauce. Cover partially and continue to cook on a medium-low heat for another 10 minutes. Sprinkle in the garam masala and mix.

5.   The whole spices in the stew are not meant to be eaten.

Royal lamb or beef with a creamy almond sauce

Shahi korma

THERE ARE many Indian dishes that were inspired, a few centuries ago, by dishes from other countries. *Shahi korma* — lamb cubes smothered in a rich almond and cream sauce — owes its ancestry to Persian food.

It could be served with rice (perhaps Spiced basmati rice, page 106) or a bread and a vegetable such as Cauliflower with potatoes (page 83). It would be good to have some kind of tomato or onion relish on the side. When I want a quick but elegant meal, I have been known to serve *shahi korma* with plain rice and a crisp green salad.

In my recipe here, I have cooked *shahi korma* the traditional way, that is on top of the cooker. If you like, you could do the final long cooking in the oven. This is particularly useful if you are making a large meal and need the top of the cooker for other dishes. Once you have combined the meat, salt, cream and water and brought it to a boil, you can cover the pan and put it in the oven instead. The cooking times and other general directions remain the same.

PREPARATION TIME: 25 minutes
COOKING TIME: about 1½ hours for lamb; about 2½ hours for beef
OVEN: 180°C, 350°F, Gas Mark 4

Serves 4-6

8 garlic cloves, peeled

1 × 2.5 cm (1 inch) cube of fresh ginger, peeled and coarsely chopped

50 g (2 oz) blanched, slivered almonds

6 tablespoons water, plus 120-250 ml (4-8 fl oz)

7 tablespoons vegetable oil

1 kg (2 lb) shoulder or leg of lamb or stewing beef, cut into 2.5 cm (1 inch) cubes

10 cardamom pods

6 cloves

2.5 cm (1 inch) piece of cinnamon stick

200 g (7 oz) onions, peeled and finely chopped

1 teaspoon ground coriander

2 teaspoons ground cumin

½ teaspoon cayenne pepper

1¼ teaspoons salt

300 ml (½ pint) single cream

¼ teaspoon garam masala (page 13)

1. Put the garlic, ginger, almonds and 6 tablespoons of water into the container of an electric blender. Blend until you have a paste.

2. Heat the oil in a wide, heavy, preferably non-stick saucepan over a medium-high flame. When it is hot, put in just enough pieces of meat so they lie, uncrowded, in a single layer. Brown the pieces of meat on all sides, then remove them with a slotted spoon and put them in a bowl. Brown all the meat this way.

3. Put the cardamom, cloves and cinnamon into the hot oil. Within seconds the cloves will expand. Now put in the onions. Stir and fry the onions until they turn a brownish colour.

4. Turn the heat down to medium. Put in the paste from the blender as well as the coriander, cumin and cayenne. Stir and fry for 3-4 minutes or until it too has browned somewhat.

5. Now put in the meat cubes as well as any liquid that might have accumulated in the meat bowl, the salt, the cream, and 120 ml (4 fl oz) water. If you are cooking beef, add another 120 ml (4 fl oz) water. Bring to a boil. Cover, turn the heat to low and simmer or cook in a preheated oven, lamb for 1 hour and beef for 2 hours, or until the meat is tender. Stir frequently during this cooking period. Skim any fat that floats to the top. Sprinkle in the garam masala and mix.

6. The whole spices in this dish are not meant to be eaten.

From the left: Royal lamb or beef with a
creamy almond sauce; Onion relish (page 125)

Delhi-style lamb cooked with potatoes

Aloo gosht

THIS IS one of the everyday meat dishes that I grew up with in Delhi. I still love its homey taste and have a particular weakness for its sauce, which seems to combine all the goodness of lamb, potatoes, tomatoes, and the cheaper, commoner Indian spices — cumin, coriander, turmeric and cayenne pepper. I like it with rice or an Indian bread and Gujerati-style green beans (page 78).

PREPARATION TIME: 35 minutes
COOKING TIME: 1½ hours

Serves 6
7 tablespoons vegetable oil
175 g (6 oz) onions, peeled and finely chopped
½-1 fresh green chilli, finely chopped
5 garlic cloves, peeled and finely chopped
1 kg (2¼ lb) boned shoulder of lamb, cut into 4 cm (1½ inch) cubes
350 g (12 oz) fresh tomatoes, peeled (page 18) and finely chopped
1 tablespoon ground cumin
2 teaspoons ground coriander
½ teaspoon ground turmeric
¼-1 teaspoon cayenne pepper
2 teaspoons salt
450 g (1 lb) medium potatoes, peeled and halved
900 ml (1½ pints) water

1. Heat the oil in a large, heavy saucepan over a high flame. When it is hot, put in the finely chopped onions, green chilli and garlic. Stir and fry until the onions have browned slightly. Put in the meat and stir it about vigorously for about 5 minutes.
2. Now put in the tomatoes, cumin, coriander, turmeric, cayenne pepper and salt. Continue to stir and cook on a high heat for 10-15 minutes or until the sauce is thick and the oil seems to separate from it.
3. Add the potatoes and the water. Cover, leaving the lid just very slightly open, and cook on a medium-low heat for about 1¼ hours or until the meat is tender and the sauce is thick.

Clockwise from the top: Delhi-style lamb cooked with potatoes; Mughlai lamb with turnips; Red split lentils with cumin seed (page 90); Gujerati-style green beans (page 78)

Mughlai lamb with turnips

Shabdeg

TURNIPS ARE perhaps the most under-rated vegetable in the world. This classical Moghul recipe calls for small, whole turnips. The turnips end up by absorbing all the delicious meat juices, turning buttery soft and yet retaining their own rather pretty shape. I like to serve this dish with Mushroom pullao (page 110) and Spicy green beans (page 78). Dal and a yogurt relish can also be added to the meal.

PREPARATION TIME: 35 minutes, plus standing
COOKING TIME: 1½ hours

Serves 6
10 small turnips, total weight 750 g (1½ lb), halved if large
2¾ teaspoons salt
450 g (1 lb) onions, peeled
8 tablespoons vegetable oil
1 kg (2¼ lb) shoulder of lamb (total weight with bone), cut into 4 cm (1½ inch) cubes
300 ml (½ pint) plain yogurt
1 × 2.5 cm (1 inch) cube of fresh ginger, peeled and very finely chopped
½ teaspoon ground turmeric
½ teaspoon cayenne pepper
1 tablespoon ground coriander
2.25 litres (4 pints) water
½ teaspoon garam masala (page 13)

Rajah Ram Singh of Kotah, Northern India, in state procession, mid 19th century

1. Peel the turnips and prick them all over with a fork. Put them in a bowl and rub them with ¾ teaspoon salt. Set aside for 1½-2 hours.
2. Cut the onions in half, lengthwise, and then crosswise into very thin slices.
3. Heat the oil in a large, wide and preferably non-stick saucepan over a medium-high flame. When it is hot, put in the onions. Stir and fry for about 12 minutes or until the onions are a reddish-brown colour. Remove the onions with a slotted spoon, squeezing out and leaving behind as much oil as you can. Spread out the onions on a plate.
4. Put the meat into the same saucepan with the yogurt, ginger and 1 teaspoon of salt.

Stir and bring to a boil. Turn the heat up high. You should, at this stage, have a fair amount of rather thin sauce. Cook on a high heat, stirring every now and then, for about 10 minutes or until the sauce is fairly thick and you just begin to see the oil. Turn the heat down a bit to medium high and continue to stir and fry for 5-7 minutes or until the meat is lightly browned and the sauce has disappeared. Turn the heat to medium-low. Put in the turmeric, cayenne and coriander. Stir for 1 minute.
5. Now put in the water and 1 teaspoon salt. Drain the turnips and add them as well. Bring the saucepan to a boil. Turn the heat to medium-high and cook, uncovered, for about 45 minutes or until you have less than a third of the liquid left. Stir several times during this cooking period.
6. Put in the browned onions and the garam masala. Stir gently to mix and turn the heat to low. Cook gently, uncovered, for 10 minutes. Stir a few times during this period, taking care not to break up the turnips.
7. Spoon off the oil that floats to the top and serve hot.

Whole leg of lamb in a spicy yogurt sauce

Raan masaledar

IF YOU ARE having guests for dinner, this might be the perfect dish to serve. It is quite impressive
—a whole leg dressed with a rich sauce, served garnished with almonds and sultanas. I often serve it
with Sweet yellow rice (page 112) and a green vegetable.

You need to buy a 2.25 kg (5 lb) leg of lamb. Get the butcher to remove the H bone and to make a
deep pocket to hold a stuffing. (You will not actually stuff the leg but most butchers seem to
understand 'stuffing' better than they do 'spice paste'.) Also, ask the butcher to cut the
protruding leg bone as close to the end of the meat as possible. This is to enable you to fit it into
your baking pan easily. Ask the butcher to remove all the fat on the outside of the leg as well as the
parchment-like skin. (You could, of course, do this yourself.)

For baking, you need a pan large enough to hold the leg easily and about 5-6 cm (2-2½ inches)
deep to hold the sauce. Ideally, the pan should have a lid but you can use aluminium foil instead.
Heatproof glass and stainless steel pans are best as they do not affect the taste of the sauce.

PREPARATION TIME: about 30 minutes, plus marinating and sitting
COOKING TIME: 2 hours   OVEN: 200°C, 400°F, Gas Mark 6

Serves 4-6	4 teaspoons ground coriander
2.5 kg (5 lb) leg of lamb, trimmed (see above)	½ teaspoon cayenne pepper
	3½ teaspoons salt
SAUCE:	½ teaspoon garam masala (page 13)
50 g (2 oz) blanched almonds	6 tablespoons vegetable oil
225 g (8 oz) onions, peeled and coarsely chopped	10 cloves
	16 cardamom pods
8 garlic cloves, peeled	5 cm (2 inch) piece of cinnamon stick
4 × 2.5 cm (1 inch) cubes of fresh ginger, peeled and coarsely chopped	10 black peppercorns
4 fresh hot green chillies, chopped	TO GARNISH:
600 ml (1 pint) plain yogurt	1 tablespoon sultanas
2 tablespoons ground cumin	15 g (½ oz) blanched, split or slivered almonds

1.   Make sure that all the fat has been trimmed from the outside of the lamb and that
most of the fell (parchment-like white skin) has
been pulled off. Put the lamb in a baking dish
made of heatproof glass or stainless steel.

2.   Put the almonds, onions, garlic, ginger,
green chillies and 3 tablespoons of the yogurt
into the container of a food processor or blender and blend until you have a paste.

3.   Put the remaining yogurt into a bowl.
Beat lightly with a fork or a whisk until it is
smooth and creamy. Add the paste from the
processor, the cumin, coriander, cayenne, salt

and garam masala. Mix.

4.   Push some of the spice paste into each
of the openings in the lamb. Be quite generous
about this. Spread the paste evenly on the
underside of the lamb (the side that originally
had less fat). Now, using a small, sharp pointed
knife (such as a paring knife), make deep
slashes in the meat and push in the spice paste
with your fingers. Turn the leg over so its outer
side (the side that was once covered with fat) is
on top. Spread a very thick layer of paste over
it. Again, make deep slashes with the knife and
push the spice paste into the slashes.

5.   Pour all the remaining spice paste over and around the meat. Cover with cling film and refrigerate for 24 hours.

6.   Take the baking dish with the meat out of the refrigerator and let the meat come to room temperature. Remove the cling film. Heat the oil in a small frying pan over a medium flame. When it is hot, put in the cloves, cardamom, cinnamon and peppercorns. When the cloves swell – this just takes a few seconds – pour the hot oil and spices over the leg of lamb.

7.   Cover the baking dish tightly either with its own lid or with a large piece of alumi-nium foil. Bake, covered, in a preheated oven for 1½ hours. Remove the foil and bake un-covered for 45 minutes. Baste 3-4 times with the sauce during this period. Scatter the sul-tanas and the almonds over the top of the lamb, or arrange them in a pattern, and bake for another 5-6 minutes.

8.   Remove the baking dish from the oven and let it sit in a warm place for 15 minutes. Take the lamb out of the pan and set it on a warm platter. Spoon off all the fat from the top of the sauce. Use a slotted spoon to remove all the whole spices from the sauce and discard them. Pour the sauce around the lamb.

From the left: Frozen spinach with potatoes (page 85);
Whole leg of lamb in a spicy yogurt sauce

From the left: Pork chipolatas cooked in an Indian style; Pork chops with chick peas

Pork chipolatas cooked in an Indian style

INDIANS CANNOT, of course, buy chipolatas in their local bazaars but here is a simple Indian-style recipe that I use when I am rushed to get dinner on the table.

PREPARATION TIME: 25 minutes   COOKING TIME: 35 minutes

Serves 4

1 × 2.5 cm (1 inch) cube of fresh ginger, peeled and coarsely chopped

3 garlic cloves, peeled

4 tablespoons water

225 g (8 oz) small courgettes

2 tablespoons vegetable oil

225 g (8 oz) pork chipolatas

100 g (4 oz) onions, peeled and chopped

1 teaspoon ground cumin

¼ teaspoon cayenne pepper

225 g (8 oz) tomatoes, peeled (page 18) and finely chopped

½ teaspoon salt

1.   Put the ginger, garlic and water into the container of a food processor or blender. Blend until you have a paste.

2.   Quarter the courgettes, lengthwise, and then cut them into 4 cm (1½ inch) lengths.

3.   Heat the oil in a large frying pan over a medium flame. Put in the chipolatas. Fry, turning them when necessary, until they have browned all over. Remove and keep on a plate.

4.   Put the onions into the same oil. Stir and fry until they begin to turn brown at the edges. Add the ginger-garlic paste. Stir and fry for 1 minute. Put in the cumin and cayenne. Stir a few times and put in the tomatoes. Stir for 1 minute. Put in the courgettes and salt. Bring to a simmer, cover, turn the heat to low and cook for 10 minutes.

5.   Cut each chipolata into 3 pieces. Add them to the pan. Cover and cook for about 5 minutes or until they have heated through.

Pork chops with chick peas

Chhole wala gosht

NORMALLY, THIS HEARTY stew-type dish is cooked with cubes of pork cut from the shoulder. I have substituted the more easily available thin-cut pork chops and added some mushrooms for good measure.

In India, we often ate this dish with what was pronounced as 'selice' and was, in reality, *slices* of white bread. (As a child, I had assumed that 'selice' was just another Indian word!) I now prefer slices from the crustier French loaf. Beside the bread, you need to serve nothing more than a simple vegetable, cooked in an Indian or English style. A simple salad would also do. This is a perfect dish for a winter's day and is best served in individual bowls or soup plates.

Dried chick peas can be cooked in many ways. You can soak them overnight before cooking them or you can follow the method that I have used here which allows the entire dish to be made in the course of a single day.

PREPARATION TIME: 30 minutes, plus standing COOKING TIME: 2¾ hours

Serves 6
225 g (8 oz) dried chick peas, rinsed and drained
1.75 litres (3 pints) water, plus 3 tablespoons
1 × 4 cm (1½ inch) cube fresh ginger, peeled and coarsely chopped
5 garlic cloves, peeled
4 tablespoons vegetable oil
1 kg (2 lb) thin-cut pork chops
8 cardamom pods
2.5 cm (1 inch) piece of cinnamon stick
2 bay leaves
1 teaspoon cumin seeds
175 g (6 oz) onions, peeled and coarsely chopped
1 tablespoon ground cumin
1 tablespoon ground coriander
1 teaspoon ground turmeric
300 g (11 oz) tomatoes, peeled (page 18) and chopped
350 g (12 oz) potatoes, peeled and cut into 2 cm (¾ inch) dice
1 tablespoon salt
275 g (10 oz) medium mushrooms, halved
about ½ teaspoon cayenne pepper

1. Put the chick peas into a saucepan. Add 1.75 litres (3 pints) water and bring to a boil. Cover, turn the heat to low and simmer for 2 minutes. Turn off the heat and let the saucepan sit, covered, for 1 hour. Bring the chick peas to a boil again. Cover, turn the heat to low and simmer for 1½ hours.

2. Put the ginger, garlic and 3 tablespoons of water into the container of a food processor or blender. Blend until you have a paste.

3. Heat the oil in a large wide saucepan over a medium-high flame. When it is hot, put in as many pork chops as the saucepan will hold in a single layer. Brown them on both sides without attempting to cook them through. Remove the chops and put them on a plate.

4. Put the cardamom, cinnamon, bay leaves and cumin seeds into the hot oil. Immediately, turn the heat down to medium-low. Stir once and put in the onions. Stir and fry the onions for 1 minute, scraping the hardened pan juices as you do so. Now put in the ginger-garlic paste and stir once. Put in the ground cumin, coriander and turmeric. Stir for 1 minute. Put in the tomatoes, potatoes, pork chops and any liquid that may have accumulated on the plate, salt, as well as the chick peas and all their cooking liquid. Stir and bring to a boil. Cover, turn the heat to low and simmer for 45 minutes. Add the mushrooms and cayenne. Cover and simmer for 15 minutes.

5. The large whole spices in this dish should not be eaten.

Goan-style hot and sour pork

Vindaloo

THE HINDUS AND MUSLIMS of India do not, generally, eat pork — but Indian Christians do. This dish, with its semi-Portuguese name suggesting that the meat is cooked with wine (or vinegar) and garlic, is a contribution from the Konkani-speaking Christians of western India. *Vindaloos*, which may be made out of lamb and beef as well, are usually very, very hot. You can control this heat by putting in just as many red chillies as you think you can manage. Serve mounds of fluffy rice on the side.

PREPARATION TIME: 35 minutes   COOKING TIME: about 1¼ hours

Akhbar, a 16th century Moghul Emperor of India, receiving the Persian ambassador

Serves 6
4 teaspoons cumin seeds
2-3 hot, dried red chillies
1 teaspoon black peppercorns
1 teaspoon cardamom seeds
7.5 cm (3 inch) piece of cinnamon stick
1½ teaspoons black mustard seeds
1 teaspoon fenugreek seeds
5 tablespoons white wine vinegar
1½-2 teaspoons salt
1 teaspoon soft light brown sugar
10 tablespoons vegetable oil
175-200 g (6-7 oz) onions, peeled and sliced into fine half-rings
4-6 tablespoons water, plus 250 ml (8 fl oz)
1 kg (2 lb) boneless pork shoulder meat, cut into 2.5 cm (1 inch) cubes
1 × 2.5 cm (1 inch) cube of fresh ginger, peeled and coarsely chopped
1 small whole head of garlic, all cloves separated and peeled
1 tablespoon ground coriander
½ teaspoon ground turmeric

1.   Grind the cumin seeds, red chillies, peppercorns, cardamom seeds, cinnamon, mustard seeds and fenugreek seeds in a coffee-grinder or other spice grinder. Put the ground spices into a bowl. Add the vinegar, salt and sugar. Mix and set aside.

From the left: Aromatic yellow rice (page 112); Goan-style hot and sour pork

2. Heat the oil in a wide, heavy saucepan over a medium flame. Put in the onions. Fry, stirring frequently, until the onions turn brown and crisp. Remove the onions with a slotted spoon and put them into the container of an electric blender or food processor. Add 2-3 tablespoons of water to the blender and purée the onions. Add this purée to the ground spices in the bowl. (This is the *vindaloo* paste. It may be made ahead of time and frozen.)

3. Dry the meat cubes with a paper towel and remove any large pieces of fat.

4. Put the ginger and garlic into the container of an electric blender or food processor. Add 2-3 tablespoons of water and blend until you have a smooth paste.

5. Heat the oil remaining in the saucepan once again over a medium-high flame. When it is hot, put in the pork cubes, a few at a time, and brown them lightly on all sides. Remove each batch with a slotted spoon and keep them in a bowl. Do all the pork this way. Now put the ginger-garlic paste into the same saucepan. Turn down the heat to medium. Stir the paste for a few seconds. Add the coriander and turmeric. Stir for another few seconds. Add the meat and any juices that may have accumulated in the bowl, the *vindaloo* paste and 250 ml (8 fl oz) water. Bring to a boil. Cover and simmer gently for 1 hour or until the pork is tender. Stir the pork gently a few times during this final cooking period.

Colva Beach, Goa

CHICKEN AND EGGS

SINCE CHICKEN is now mass produced — and fairly cheap — its status has been greatly reduced. This saddens me. I was brought up thinking of chicken as something special and have never managed to get over thinking so; besides, I like chicken. And there are such wonderful ways to cook it, from the simple *Masaledar murghi* (Spicy baked chicken) to the elegant *Makkhani murghi* (Chicken in a butter sauce) and the very impressive *Murgh musallam* (Whole chicken baked in aluminium foil). If you are on a diet, you can eat *Tandoori murghi* (Tandoori-style chicken), which is cooked without fat and when you want to indulge yourself, you can dine on *Shahjahani murghi* (Mughlai chicken with almonds and raisins).

There are two things to remember when cooking Indian-style chicken dishes. The first is that we nearly always skin the chicken before we cook it. The second is that, for most of our dishes, we cut up the chicken into fairly small pieces. Legs, for example, are always separated into drumsticks and thighs and each breast is cut into 2-3 pieces. Wings and backs are similarly cut up.

When one of my recipes calls for chicken pieces, you can either buy a whole 1.35-1.5 kg (3-3½ lb) chicken and cut it up yourself using a sharp knife and a cleaver or else you can buy chicken joints — the ones you prefer — and cut them up further, if necessary. I happen to have a family in which four members like dark meat and one only likes breast meat (unless it is a roast, when we all prefer breast meat). This does not make life easy, so I frequently resort to buying joints.

I have a few egg recipes in this chapter as well. If you are looking for a new, spicier approach to eggs, try *Ekoori* (Spicy scrambled eggs) cooked with fresh green coriander and tomato or the pie-like *Parsi omlate* (Vegetable omelette), seasoned with cumin and green chillies.

45

Bombay-style chicken with red split lentils

Murghi aur masoor dal

THIS DISH, in which chicken is combined with red lentils, is really like a hearty stew, just perfect for cold winter days. You could add vegetables to it as well, such as shelled peas or 1 cm (½ inch) lengths of green beans. If you do this, put in the vegetables at about the same time as you put in the lemon juice.

Traditionally, rice is served on the side but, if you like, you could have this dish with thickly cut slices of some dark, crusty bread.

PREPARATION TIME: 40 minutes
COOKING TIME: about 1½ hours

Serves 6-7
250 g (9 oz) red split lentils, washed, and drained
75 g (3 oz) onion, peeled and chopped
½-1 fresh hot green chilli, finely sliced
2 teaspoons ground cumin
½ teaspoon ground turmeric
1 teaspoon very finely chopped, peeled ginger
1.5 litres (2½ pints) water
about 1.5 kg (3 lb) jointed chicken pieces, skinned
2¼ teaspoons salt
2 tablespoons vegetable oil
1 teaspoon cumin seeds
2-4 garlic cloves, peeled and finely chopped
¼-¾ teaspoon cayenne pepper
2 tablespoons lemon juice
½ teaspoon sugar
¼ teaspoon garam masala (page 13)
3 tablespoons chopped fresh coriander, to garnish

1. Combine the lentils, onion, green chilli, ground cumin, turmeric, half of the chopped ginger and 1.5 litres (2½ pints) water in a big, heavy saucepan. Bring to a simmer, cover, leaving the lid very slightly open, and cook on a low heat for 45 minutes. Add the chicken and the salt. Mix and bring to a boil. Cover, turn the heat to low and simmer gently for 25-30 minutes or until the chicken is tender.

2. Heat the oil in a small frying pan over a medium flame. When it is hot, put in the cumin seeds. As soon as the seeds begin to sizzle – this just takes a few seconds – put in the remaining ½ teaspoon chopped ginger and the garlic. Fry until the garlic turns slightly brown. Now put in the cayenne pepper. Lift up the frying pan immediately and pour its entire contents – oil and spices – into the saucepan with the chicken and lentils. Also, at the same time, add the lemon juice, sugar and garam masala. Stir to mix and cook on a medium-low flame for another 5 minutes.

3. Sprinkle the fresh coriander over the top just before you serve.

Spicy baked chicken

Masaledar murghi

HERE IS one of those easy chicken dishes that can be prepared almost effortlessly. There is a marinating period, though, of about 3 hours. This chicken has a very red look which it gets

from ground, hot red chillies. To get the same effect – and not all of the heat – you can combine paprika with cayenne pepper in any proportion that you like as long as the total quantity is about 1½ tablespoons.
I like to serve this chicken with Rice with peas (page 109) and Red split lentils with cumin seed (page 90).

PREPARATION TIME: 35 minutes, plus marinating
COOKING TIME: about 45 minutes
OVEN: 200°C, 400°F, Gas Mark 6

Serves 6
1 tablespoon ground cumin
1 tablespoon paprika
1½ teaspoons cayenne pepper (see above)
1 tablespoon ground turmeric
1-1½ teaspoons freshly ground black pepper
2½-3 teaspoons salt – or to taste
2-3 garlic cloves, peeled and mashed to a pulp
6 tablespoons lemon juice
1.5 kg (3½ lb) jointed chicken pieces
3 tablespoons vegetable oil

1.   Combine the cumin, paprika, cayenne, turmeric, black pepper, salt, garlic and lemon juice in a bowl. Mix well. Rub this mixture over the chicken pieces, pushing the paste inside any flaps and openings that you can find. Stuff some paste along the bone of the drumsticks.
2.   Spread the chicken pieces in a shallow baking tray, skin side down, and set aside in a cool place for 3 hours. (Longer will not hurt, just cover the chicken with cling film to prevent it from drying out.)
3.   Brush the tops of the chicken pieces with the oil. Put the chicken in a preheated oven and bake for 20 minutes. Turn the chicken pieces over and bake another 25 minutes or until the chicken is tender. Baste the chicken pieces with the drippings 3-4 times.
4.   Arrange the chicken pieces on a platter, pour the sauce over them and serve at once.

From the top:
Bombay-style chicken with red split lentils;
Spicy baked chicken and Rice with peas (page 109)

Tandoori-style chicken

Tandoori murghi

I HAVE, I think, found a way to make tandoori-style chicken without a *tandoor*! The *tandoor*, as I am sure you all know by now, is a vat-shaped clay oven, heated with charcoal or wood. The heat inside builds up to such an extent that small whole chickens, skewered and thrust into it, cook in about 10 minutes. This fierce heat seals the juices of the bird and keeps it moist while an earlier marinating process ensures that the chicken is tender and well flavoured. The result is quite spectacular.

To approximate a *tandoor*, I use an ordinary oven, preheated to its maximum temperature. Then, instead of cooking a whole bird, I use serving-sized pieces — legs that are cut into two and breasts that are halved. The cooking time is not 10 minutes because home ovens do not get as hot as *tandoors*. Still, breasts cook in about 15-20 minutes and legs in 20-25 minutes.

Tandoori chicken may, of course, be served just the way it comes out of the oven with a few wedges of lemon, or it can, without much effort, be transformed into *Makkhani murghi* (page 50) by smothering it with a rich butter-cream-tomato sauce. Both dishes are excellent for dinner parties as most of the work can be done a day ahead of time. The chicken is marinated the night before so all you have to do on the day of the party is to cook it in the oven for a brief 20-25 minutes just before you sit down to eat. If you wish to make the sauce, all the ingredients for it except the butter may be combined in a bowl the day before and refrigerated. After that, the sauce cooks in less than 5 minutes and involves only one step — heating it. Both these chicken dishes may be served with rice or naan and a green bean or cauliflower dish.

The traditional orange colour of cooked tandoori chicken comes from food colouring. You may or may not want to use it. If you do, mix yellow and red liquid food colours to get a bright orange shade. If your red is very dark, use only ½ tablespoon.

PREPARATION TIME: 1 hour, plus standing and marinating
COOKING TIME: 25 minutes
OVEN: 240°C, 475°F, Gas Mark 9

Serves 4-6	1 × 2 cm (¾ inch) cube of fresh ginger, peeled and quartered
1.25 kg (2½ lb) jointed chicken pieces, skinned (you may use legs, breasts or a combination of the two)	½ fresh, hot green chilli, roughly sliced
1 teaspoon salt	2 teaspoons garam masala (page 13)
1 juicy lemon	3 tablespoons yellow liquid food colouring mixed with ½-1½ tablespoons red liquid food colouring (optional) (see note above)
450 ml (¾ pint) plain yogurt	
½ medium onion, peeled and quartered	
1 garlic clove, peeled	lime wedges

1. Cut each leg and each breast into 2 pieces. Cut 2 long slits on each side of each part of the legs. The slits should never start at an edge and they should be deep enough to reach the bone. Cut similar slits on the meaty side of each breast piece.
2. Spread the chicken pieces out on one or two large platters. Sprinkle ½ teaspoon salt

and squeeze the juice from three-quarters of the lemon over them. Lightly rub the salt and lemon juice into the slits. Turn the chicken pieces over and do the same on the other side with the remaining salt and lemon juice. Set the chicken pieces aside for 20 minutes.
3. Combine the yogurt, onion, garlic, ginger, green chilli and garam masala in the con-

tainer of an electric blender or food processor. Blend until you have a smooth paste. Empty the paste into a strainer set over a large ceramic or stainless steel bowl. Push the paste through.

4. Brush the chicken pieces on both sides with the food colouring, if using, and then put them with any accumulated juices and any remaining food colouring into the bowl with the marinade. Mix well, making sure that the marinade goes into the slits in the chicken. Cover and refrigerate for 6-24 hours (the longer the better).

5. Take the chicken pieces out of the bowl, shaking off as much of the marinade as possible. Arrange them in a large shallow baking tray in a single layer. Bake for 20-25 minutes or until just done. Test the chicken with a fork just to be sure. Serve hot, with lime wedges.

From the left: Cauliflower with potatoes (page 83); Tandoori chicken; Naan (page 99)

Chicken in a butter sauce

Makkhani murghi

THE SAUCE in this dish should be folded into melted butter at the very last minute as it tends to separate otherwise. However, you can combine all the ingredients except the butter up to a day ahead of time and refrigerate them until they are needed.
This is a wonderfully simple but spectacular dish in which the Tandoori-style chicken of the preceding recipe is transformed with a sauce.

PREPARATION TIME: 20 minutes, plus cooking the Tandoori-style chicken
COOKING TIME: 5 minutes

Serves 4-6

4 tablespoons tomato purée

1 × 2.5 cm (1 inch) cube of fresh ginger, peeled and very finely grated

300 ml (½ pint) single cream

1 teaspoon garam masala (page 13)

¾ teaspoon salt

¼ teaspoon sugar

1 fresh hot green chilli, finely chopped

¼ teaspoon cayenne pepper

1 tablespoon very finely chopped fresh coriander

4 teaspoons lemon juice

1 teaspoon ground roasted cumin seeds (page 13)

100 g (4 oz) unsalted butter

tandoori-style chicken, freshly cooked according to the preceding recipe

1.   Put the tomato purée in a clear measuring jug. Add water slowly, mixing as you go, to make up 250 ml (8 fl oz) of tomato sauce. Add the ginger, cream, garam masala, salt, sugar, chilli, cayenne, fresh coriander, lemon juice and ground roasted cumin seeds. Mix well.
2.   Heat the butter in a large frying pan. When it has melted, add the contents of the measuring jug. Bring to a simmer and cook on medium heat for 1 minute, mixing in the butter as you do so. Add the chicken pieces (but not their accumulated juices). Stir once and put the chicken pieces on a warm serving platter. Extra sauce should be spooned over the top.

Lemony chicken with fresh coriander

Hare masale wali murghi

HERE IS a delightful lemony, gingery dish that requires quite a lot of fresh coriander. It is a great favourite with our family. I generally serve it with Spiced basmati rice (page 106).

PREPARATION TIME: 30 minutes
COOKING TIME: 40 minutes

Serves 6

2 × 2.5 cm (1 inch) cubes of fresh ginger, peeled and coarsely chopped

4 tablespoons water, plus 150 ml (¼ pint)

6 tablespoons vegetable oil

1.25 kg (2½ lb) chicken pieces, skinned

5 garlic cloves, peeled and chopped

200 g (7 oz) fresh coriander, very finely chopped

½-1 fresh hot green chilli, very finely chopped

¼ teaspoon cayenne pepper

2 teaspoons ground cumin

1 teaspoon ground coriander

½ teaspoon ground turmeric

1 teaspoon salt — or to taste

2 tablespoons lemon juice

From the top: Lemony chicken with fresh coriander; Chicken in a butter sauce; Spiced basmati rice (page 106)

1.   Put the ginger and 4 tablespoons of water into the container of an electric blender. Blend until you have a paste.

2.   Heat the oil in a wide, heavy, preferably non-stick, saucepan over a medium-high flame. When it is hot, put in as many chicken pieces as the saucepan will hold in a single layer and brown them on both sides. Remove the chicken pieces with a slotted spoon and put them into a bowl. Brown all the chicken pieces in this way.

3.   Put the garlic into the same hot oil. As soon as the pieces turn a medium brown colour, turn the heat to medium and pour in the paste from the blender. Stir and fry it for 1 minute. Now add the fresh coriander, green chilli, cayenne, cumin, coriander, turmeric and salt. Stir and cook for 1 minute.

4.   Put in all the chicken pieces as well as any liquid that might have accumulated in the chicken bowl. Also add 150 ml (¼ pint) water and the lemon juice. Stir and bring to a boil. Cover tightly, turn the heat to low and cook for 15 minutes. Turn the chicken pieces over. Cover again and cook for another 10-15 minutes or until the chicken is tender. If the sauce is too thin, uncover the saucepan and boil some of it away over a slightly higher heat.

51

Chicken in a red sweet pepper sauce

Lal masale wali murghi

MANY OF THE MEAT, poultry and fish dishes from India's west coast have thick, red-looking sauces. The main ingredient, which provides both the texture and the colour, are red chillies — either fresh or dried. It is almost impossible to find the correct variety in Britain — one that is bright red and just mildly hot — but a combination of red peppers and cayenne pepper works exceedingly well!
I like to serve this dish with Aromatic yellow rice (page 112) and
Yogurt with aubergines (page 119).

PREPARATION TIME: 30 minutes   COOKING TIME: 35 minutes

Serves 4

1 kg (2¼ lb) jointed chicken pieces (legs or breasts), skinned
100 g (4 oz) onions, peeled and coarsely chopped
1 × 2.5 cm (1 inch) cube of fresh ginger, peeled and coarsely chopped
3 garlic cloves, peeled
25 g (1 oz) blanched, slivered almonds
350 g (12 oz) red sweet peppers, trimmed, seeded, and coarsely chopped
1 tablespoon ground cumin
2 teaspoons ground coriander
½ teaspoon ground turmeric
⅛-½ teaspoon cayenne pepper
2 teaspoons salt
7 tablespoons vegetable oil
250 ml (8 fl oz) water
2 tablespoons lemon juice
½ teaspoon coarsely ground black pepper

1.   Using a sharp knife, divide the chicken legs into thighs and drumsticks and cut each breast into 2 pieces.
2.   Combine the onions, ginger, garlic, almonds, peppers, cumin, coriander, turmeric, cayenne and salt in the container of a food processor or blender. Blend, pushing down with a rubber spatula whenever you need to, until you have a paste.
3.   Put the oil in a large, wide, and prefer-ably non-stick saucepan and heat it over a medium-high flame. When it is hot, pour in all the paste from the food processor or blender. Stir and fry the paste for 10-12 minutes or until you can see the oil forming tiny bubbles around it.
4.   Put in the chicken with the water, lemon juice and black pepper. Stir to mix and bring to a boil. Cover, turn the heat to low and simmer gently for 25 minutes or until the chicken is tender. Stir a few times during this cooking period.

Chicken in a red sweet pepper sauce

Chicken in a fried onion sauce

Pictured on
page 54

Murghi rasedar

THIS IS how I cook the dish that my children refer to as our 'everyday' chicken. We tend to eat it with Plain basmati rice (page 107) and Carrot and onion salad (page 123).

PREPARATION TIME: 35 minutes
COOKING TIME: about 40 minutes

Serves 4-6

1.25 kg (2½ lb) chicken pieces, skinned

350 g (12 oz) onions, peeled

1 × 4 cm (1½ inch) cube of fresh ginger, peeled and coarsely chopped

6 garlic cloves, peeled

2 tablespoons water, plus 600 ml (1 pint)

7 tablespoons vegetable oil

1 tablespoon ground coriander

1 tablespoon ground cumin

½ teaspoon ground turmeric

¼-½ teaspoon cayenne pepper

4 tablespoons plain yogurt

225 g (8 oz) tomatoes, peeled (page 18) and very finely chopped

2 teaspoons salt

½ teaspoon garam masala (page 13)

1 tablespoon finely chopped fresh coriander (parsley may be substituted)

1. Cut the chicken into serving pieces. Whole legs should be separated into drumsticks and thighs. Each breast should be cut into 2-3 pieces, depending on size.
2. Chop 175 g (6 oz) of the onions coarsely. Cut the remaining onions into halves lengthwise, and then into very thin slices.

3. Put the chopped onions, ginger, garlic and 2 tablespoons of the water into the container of a food processor or blender. Blend until you have a paste.
4. Heat the oil in a large, wide saucepan or a large, deep, preferably non-stick, frying pan over a medium flame. When it is hot, put in the sliced onions. Stir and fry the onions until they are a deep, reddish-brown colour. Remove the onions with a slotted spoon, squeezing out and leaving behind as much of the oil as possible. Put the onions into a bowl and set aside.
5. Take the saucepan off the flame. Put in the blended paste (keep your face averted). Put the saucepan back on the heat. Stir and fry the paste for about 3-4 minutes until it is brown. Now put in the coriander, cumin, turmeric and cayenne and stir once. Put in 1 tablespoon of the yogurt. Stir for about 30 seconds or until it has been incorporated into the sauce. Add all the yogurt this way, 1 tablespoon at a time. Put in the chicken pieces and stir them around for a minute.
6. Pour in 600 ml (1 pint) of the water, add the tomatoes and salt. Stir to mix and bring to a simmer. Cover, turn the heat to low and cook for 20 minutes. Sprinkle in the garam masala and the fried onions. Mix. Cook, un-covered, on a medium heat for 7-8 minutes or until the sauce reduces and thickens.
7. Skim the fat and put the chicken into a warm serving dish. Sprinkle the fresh coriander or parsley over the top.

Clockwise from the left: Yogurt with cucumber and mint (page 119); Chicken in a fried onion sauce (page 53) and Carrot and onion salad (page 123); Poppadum (page 130); Mughlai chicken with almonds and sultanas and Spiced basmati rice (page 106)

Mughlai chicken with almonds and sultanas

Shahjahani murghi

THIS ELEGANT mild dish is very suitable for dinner parties. It could be accompanied by Spiced basmati rice (page 106), Cauliflower with potatoes (page 83) and Yogurt with cucumber and mint (page 119).

PREPARATION TIME: 45 minutes   COOKING TIME: 50 minutes

Serves 6
1 × 2.5 cm (1 inch) cube of fresh ginger, peeled and coarsely chopped
8-9 garlic cloves, peeled
6 tablespoons blanched, slivered almonds
4 tablespoons water
7 tablespoons vegetable oil
1.5 kg (3 lb) chicken pieces, skinned
10 cardamom pods
2.5 cm (1 inch) piece of cinnamon stick
2 bay leaves
5 cloves
200 g (7 oz) onions, peeled and finely chopped
2 teaspoons ground cumin
1/8-1/2 teaspoon cayenne pepper
7 tablespoons plain yogurt
1½ teaspoons salt
300 ml (½ pint) single cream
1-2 tablespoons sultanas
¼ teaspoon garam masala (page 13)

1. Put the ginger, garlic, 4 tablespoons of the almonds and the water into the container of an electric blender or food processor and blend until you have a paste.

2. Heat the oil in a wide, preferably non-stick, saucepan over a medium-high flame. When it is hot, put in as many chicken pieces as the pan will hold in a single layer. Let the chicken pieces turn golden brown on the bottom. Now turn all the pieces over and brown the other side. Remove the chicken pieces with a slotted spoon and put them in a bowl. Brown all the chicken pieces in this way.

3. Put the cardamom, cinnamon, bay leaves and cloves into the same hot oil. Stir and fry them for a few seconds. Now put in the onions. Stir and fry the onions for 3-4 minutes or until they are lightly browned. Put in the paste from the blender, the cumin and cayenne. Stir and fry for 2-3 minutes or until the oil seems to separate from the spice mixture and the spices are lightly browned. Add 1 tablespoon of the yogurt. Stir and fry it for about 30 seconds. Now add another tablespoon of yogurt. Keep doing this until all the yogurt has been incorporated.

4. Put in the chicken pieces, any liquid that might have accumulated in the chicken bowl, the cream and salt. Bring to a simmer. Cover, turn the heat to low and cook gently for 20 minutes. Add the sultanas and turn over the chicken pieces. Cover and cook for another 10 minutes or until the chicken is tender. Add the garam masala. Stir to mix.

5. Place the remaining almonds on a baking tray and put them under a preheated grill until they brown lightly. You will have to toss them frequently. Sprinkle these almonds over the chicken when you serve. Extra fat may be spooned off the top just before serving.

6. The whole spices in the dish are not meant to be eaten.

Goan-style chicken with roasted coconut

Shakoothi

I JUST LOVE this dish. I ate it for the first time in balmy, palm-fringed, coastal Goa, and have been hoarding the recipe ever since. Even though there are several steps to the recipe, it is not at all hard to put together, especially if you have grated coconut sitting around in the freezer, as I always have. I am now in the habit of buying two or three coconuts whenever I see any good ones. I grate them as soon as I get home (for instructions, see page 12) and then store the grated flesh in flattened plastic packets. Thawing takes no time at all. This way, I am always ready, not only to make *Shakoothi*, but to sprinkle fresh coconut over meats and vegetables whenever I want to. You could serve this dish with Plain long-grain rice (page 107), Spicy green beans (page 78) and Onion relish (page 125).

PREPARATION TIME: 1 hour

COOKING TIME: 55 minutes

Serves 4-5

1½ tablespoons coriander seeds

1½ teaspoons cumin seeds

1 teaspoon black mustard seeds

2.5 cm (1 inch) piece of cinnamon stick, broken up into 3-4 pieces

4 cloves

¼ teaspoon black peppercorns

about ⅙ of a nutmeg

1 dried hot red chilli (remove the seeds if you want it mild)

enough grated fresh coconut (page 12) to fill a glass measuring jug to the 450 ml (¾ pint) level

6-8 garlic cloves, peeled

1 × 2.5 cm (1 inch) cube of fresh ginger, peeled and coarsely chopped

½-1 fresh hot green chilli

4 tablespoons water, plus 300 ml (½ pint)

4 tablespoons vegetable oil

175 g (6 oz) onions, peeled and minced

1 kg (2¼ lb) jointed chicken pieces, skinned

1½ teaspoons salt

1. Put the coriander seeds, cumin seeds, mustard seeds, cinnamon, cloves, peppercorns, nutmeg and red chilli into a small, preferably cast-iron, frying pan. Place the pan over a medium flame. Now quickly 'dry-roast' the spices, stirring them frequently until they emit a very pleasant 'roasted' aroma. Empty the spices into a clean coffee grinder or spice grinder and grind until fine. Take the spices out and put them in a bowl.

2. Put the coconut into the same frying pan and dry-roast it over a medium flame, stirring it all the time. The coconut should pick up lots of brown flecks and also smell 'roasted'. Put the coconut into the bowl with the other dry roasted spices.

3. Put the garlic, ginger and green chilli into the container of an electric blender, along with 4 tablespoons of the water. Blend them together until you have a paste.

4. Heat the oil in a 25-30 cm (10-12 inch) frying pan or sauté pan over a medium-high flame. When it is hot, put in the onions. Stir and fry them until they pick up brown spots. Now pour in the garlic-ginger mixture from the blender and stir once. Turn the heat to medium. Put in the chicken pieces, salt and the spice-coconut mixture in the bowl. Stir and fry the chicken for 3-4 minutes or until it loses its pinkness and turns slightly brown. Add 300 ml (½ pint) water and bring to a simmer. Cover tightly, turn the heat to low, and cook for 25-30 minutes or until the chicken is tender. Stir a few times during this cooking period, making sure that you turn over each piece of chicken so that it gets evenly coloured.

Chicken with tomatoes and garam masala

Timatar murghi

THIS SIMPLE chicken dish is a great favourite with our children. I generally serve it with Plain long-grain rice (page 107) and Whole green lentils with garlic and onion (page 92).

PREPARATION TIME: 40 minutes   COOKING TIME: 35 minutes

Serves 6
5 tablespoons vegetable oil
¾ teaspoon cumin seeds
2.5 cm (1 inch) piece of cinnamon stick
6 cardamom pods
2 bay leaves
¼ teaspoon whole black peppercorns
175 g (6 oz) onions, peeled and finely chopped
6-7 garlic cloves, peeled and finely chopped
1 × 2.5 cm (1 inch) cube of fresh ginger, peeled and finely chopped
450 g (1 lb) fresh tomatoes, peeled (page 18) and finely chopped
1.5 kg (3 lb) chicken pieces, skinned
1½ teaspoons salt
⅛-½ teaspoon cayenne pepper
½ teaspoon garam masala (page 13)

1.   Heat the oil in a large wide saucepan over a medium-high flame. When it is hot, put in the cumin seeds, cinnamon, cardamom, bay leaves and peppercorns. Stir once and then put in the onions, garlic and ginger. Stir this mixture around until the onion picks up brown specks. Put in the tomatoes, chicken, salt and cayenne pepper. Stir to mix and bring to a boil.

2.   Cover tightly, turn the heat to low and simmer for 25 minutes or until the chicken is tender. Stir a few times during this cooking period. Remove the lid and turn up the heat to medium. Sprinkle in the garam masala and cook, stirring gently, for about 5 minutes in order to reduce the liquid somewhat.

3.   The whole spices in this dish should not be eaten.

From the top: Chicken with tomatoes and garam masala; Goan-style chicken with roasted coconut and Plain long-grain rice (page 107)

57

Whole chicken baked in aluminium foil

Murgh musallam

OVER THE YEARS, as I am more and more rushed for time, I find myself simplifying some of my own recipes. The traditional *murgh musallam* recipe, for example, is quite a complicated one. I now cook it relatively simply, by smothering a marinated bird with a spice paste, wrapping it in foil and popping it into the oven. It works beautifully.
I like to serve this dish with Mushroom pullao (page 110), Frozen spinach with potatoes (page 85) and Yogurt with cucumber and mint (page 119).

PREPARATION TIME: 45 minutes, plus marinating
COOKING TIME: about 1¾ hours
OVEN: 180°C, 350°F, Gas Mark 4

Serves 4-6
1.5 kg (3½ lb) chicken
225 g (8 oz) onions
4 garlic cloves, peeled
1 × 4 cm (1½ inch) cube of fresh ginger, peeled and coarsely chopped
25 g (1 oz) blanched, slivered almonds
2 teaspoons ground cumin
2 teaspoons ground coriander
½ teaspoon ground turmeric
1 tablespoon ground paprika
¼ teaspoon cayenne pepper
1½ teaspoons salt
8 tablespoons vegetable oil
2 tablespoons lemon juice
½ teaspoon coarsely ground black pepper
½ teaspoon garam masala (page 13)
MARINADE:
1 × 2.5 cm (1 inch) cube of fresh ginger, peeled and coarsely chopped
2 large garlic cloves, peeled
6 tablespoons plain yogurt
½ teaspoon ground turmeric
1¼ teaspoons salt
¼-½ teaspoon cayenne pepper
freshly ground black pepper

1. Make the marinade: Put the ginger, garlic and 3 tablespoons of the yogurt into the container of a food processor or blender. Blend, pushing down with a rubber spatula whenever you need to, until you have a paste. Add the turmeric, salt, cayenne and black pepper. Blend for 1 second to mix. Empty the marinade into a bowl. (Do not wash out the food processor or blender yet.) Add the remaining 3 tablespoons of the yogurt to the marinade and beat it in with a fork.

2. Skin the entire chicken with the exception of the wing tips. Skin the neck. Put the

Two princes conversing in a garden at night,
Northern India, 17th century

CHICKEN AND EGGS
Clockwise from the top: Yogurt with cucumber and mint (page 119); Whole chicken baked in aluminium foil;
Frozen spinach with potatoes (page 85); Mushroom pullao (page 110)

chicken, breast upwards, on a platter and put the giblets beside it. Rub the chicken inside and out, and the giblets, with the marinade. Set aside, unrefrigerated, for 2 hours.
3.   Meanwhile, put the onions, garlic, ginger and almonds into the food processor or blender. Blend, pushing down with a rubber spatula whenever you need to, until you have a paste. Add the cumin, coriander, turmeric, paprika, cayenne and salt. Blend again to mix.
4.   Heat the oil in a large non-stick saucepan over a medium-high flame. Put in the paste from the food processor or blender. Fry, stirring, for 8-9 minutes. Add the lemon juice,

black pepper and garam masala. Mix. Turn off the heat and let the paste cool.
5.   Remove the chicken from the marinade and spread out a piece of aluminium foil, large enough to enclose the chicken. Put the chicken, breast upwards, in the centre of the foil and put the giblets beside it. Rub the chicken, inside and out, and the giblets, with the fried spice paste. Bring the ends of the foil towards the centre to form a tight packet. All 'seams' should be 5 cm (2 inches) above the 'floor' of the packet. Put the wrapped chicken, breast up, on a baking tray and bake in a preheated oven for 1½ hours or until tender.

Vegetable omelette

Parsi omlate

THE PARSIS who settled on India's west coast around the Bombay area, came originally from Persia over a thousand years ago. Even though they have proudly retained their religion, Zoroastrianism, they have been unafraid to let their adopted country or, for that matter, British colonialists, influence them in their choice of dress, language and food. The Parsi culinary tradition is unique, borrowing freely as it does from Gujeratis, Maharashtrians and the English. But there is a Persian streak in there as well. This can best be seen in the fondness for eggs and the abundance of egg dishes — eggs over fried okra, eggs over matchstick potatoes, eggs over tomato chutney — the list is long. Parsis also make all kinds of omelettes. Some are folded in the traditional way but many others are round and pie-like. The recipe here is for a pie-like omelette, filled with vegetables.

This omelette has become one of my favourite brunch dishes now. It may be served, Western-style, with a salad, French bread and white wine, or it may be served Indian-style, with a stack of parathas or toast, Tomato, onion and green coriander relish (page 124), and steaming hot tea.

To make this omelette properly, it really helps to have a non-stick frying pan. The one I use measures 19 cm (7½ inches) across at the bottom, curving up to 25 cm (10 inches) across at the top. It is 5 cm (2 inches) deep. Your pan may have a somewhat different shape. It does not really matter. Just remember that the pie-shaped omelette rises slightly as it is cooking so a little space has to be left at the top. You also need a lid. If your frying pan does not have one, use aluminium foil.

PREPARATION TIME: 30 minutes, plus standing
COOKING TIME: 30 minutes

Serves 6
450 g (1 lb) courgettes
1¾ teaspoons salt
5 tablespoons vegetable oil
100 g (4 oz) onions, peeled and finely chopped
150 g (5 oz) potatoes, peeled and cut into 5 mm (¼ inch) dice
1-3 fresh hot green chillies, finely chopped
200 g (7 oz) tomatoes, chopped
1½ teaspoons ground cumin
⅛-¼ teaspoon cayenne pepper, optional
freshly ground black pepper
9 eggs (size 1)
3 tablespoons finely chopped fresh coriander (or use parsley)
¼ teaspoon baking soda

1. Trim and discard the ends of the courgettes and then grate them coarsely. Put the grated courgettes into a bowl. Sprinkle ¾ teaspoon salt over them and mix thoroughly. Set aside for 30 minutes. Squeeze all the liquid out of the grated courgettes and then separate the strands so they are no longer bunched up.

2. Heat 3 tablespoons of the oil in a non-stick frying pan (see note at the top of the recipe) over a medium flame. When it is hot, put in the onions. Stir and fry for 1 minute. Now put in the potatoes and the green chillies. Stir and fry for about 5 minutes or until the potato pieces are just about tender. Add the courgettes, tomatoes, cumin, 1 teaspoon salt, cayenne and a generous amount of black pepper. Stir and cook for 2-3 minutes or until the tomato pieces are soft. Set aside to cool.

3. Break the eggs into a bowl and beat them well. Empty the cooled vegetable mixture into the beaten eggs and add the fresh coriander. Stir to mix. Sprinkle in the baking soda, making sure that it is lump-free. Mix again.

4. Wipe out the frying pan with a paper towel. Pour in the remaining oil and set to heat

Clockwise from top left: Spicy scrambled eggs (page 62); Vinegared eggs (page 62); Vegetable omelette; Paratha (page 98)

on a low flame. When it is hot, pour in the egg mixture. Cover and cook on low heat for 15 minutes. Remove the lid and place the pan 5-7 cms (2-3 inches) beneath a preheated hot grill and cook for about 4-5 minutes until the top of the omelette is golden brown. Transfer the omelette to a serving platter. Serve hot, warm or at room temperature.

Pictured on
page 61

Vinegared eggs

Baida vindaloo

THIS VINEGARY hard-boiled egg dish is almost like a pickle and perfect for taking out on picnics. It is, like all Goan-style *vindaloo* dishes, tart, hot, garlicky and just very slightly sweet. I have lessened the tartness somewhat by cooking the eggs in a mixture of vinegar and water instead of just vinegar. Use the mildest vinegar that you can find. In this recipe, you may use anywhere from 6 to 8 eggs without having to alter any of the other ingredients. You could serve this dish with rice or an Indian bread. Cauliflower with potatoes (page 83) would make a nice accompaniment.

PREPARATION TIME: 20 minutes
COOKING TIME: 30 minutes

Serves 3-4
4 garlic cloves, peeled and crushed
1 × 2.5 cm (1 inch) cube of fresh ginger, peeled and very finely grated
⅛-½ teaspoon cayenne pepper
2 teaspoons paprika
1½ teaspoons ground cumin
1¼ teaspoons salt
1½ tablespoons brown sugar
2 tablespoons mild white vinegar, plus 120 ml (4 fl oz)
3 tablespoons vegetable oil
2.5 cm (1 inch) piece of cinnamon stick
225 g (8 oz) onions, peeled and finely chopped
½ teaspoon garam masala (page 13)
175 ml (6 fl oz) water
6-8 hard-boiled eggs, peeled and cut crosswise into halves

1.   Combine the garlic, ginger, cayenne, paprika, cumin, salt, sugar and 2 tablespoons of vinegar in a cup or small bowl. Mix well.
2.   Heat the oil in a medium-sized frying pan over medium heat. When it is hot, put in the cinnamon stick. Let it sizzle for a few seconds. Now put in all the onions. Stir and fry for about 5 minutes or until the onions have softened. Put in the paste from the cup as well as the garam masala. Stir and fry for 2 minutes. Add the remaining vinegar and the water. Stir to mix and bring to a simmer.
3.   Put all the egg halves into the frying pan in a single layer, cut side up, and spoon the sauce over them. Cook on medium heat for about 5 minutes or until the sauce has thickened. Spoon the sauce frequently over the eggs as you do so.

Spicy scrambled eggs

Pictured on
page 61

Ekoori

EKOORI is the Parsi name for them but scrambled eggs, cooked in a similar style, are eaten all over India. Eat them with toast or any Indian bread.

PREPARATION TIME: 20 minutes
COOKING TIME: about 12 minutes

Serves 4
3 tablespoons unsalted butter or vegetable oil
1 small onion, peeled and finely chopped
½ teaspoon peeled and very finely grated fresh ginger
½-1 fresh hot green chilli, finely chopped
1 tablespoon very finely chopped fresh coriander
⅛ teaspoon ground turmeric
½ teaspoon ground cumin
1 small tomato, peeled (page 18) and chopped
6 large eggs, lightly beaten
salt
freshly ground pepper

1.   Melt the butter in a medium sized, preferably non-stick, frying pan over a medium heat. Put in the onion and fry gently until it is soft. Add the ginger, chilli, fresh coriander,

turmeric, cumin and tomato. Stir and cook for 3-4 minutes or until the tomatoes are soft.

2.   Put in the beaten eggs. Season them lightly with salt and pepper. Stir the eggs gently until they form soft, thick curds. Cook the scrambled eggs to any consistency you like.

Hard-boiled eggs in a spicy cream sauce

Malaidar unday

THIS DELICIOUS egg dish can be put together rather quickly and is just perfect for brunches, light lunches, and suppers. You could serve toast on the side or, if you like, rice and a crisp salad. If you prefer to serve a more traditional Indian meal, then Parathas (page 98) or Spiced basmati rice (page 106) and Gujerati-style green beans (page 78) would be suitable accompaniments. This recipe calls for a small amount of chicken stock. If you have some home-made stock handy, fine. Otherwise, use stock made with a cube, but adjust your salt as cube stock can be salty.

PREPARATION TIME: 20 minutes   COOKING TIME: 25 minutes

Serves 3-4

3 tablespoons vegetable oil

50 g (2 oz) onion, peeled and chopped

1 × 2.5 cm (1 inch) cube of fresh ginger, peeled and finely grated

½-1 fresh hot green chilli, finely chopped

300 ml (½ pint) single cream

1 tablespoon lemon juice

1 teaspoon ground, roasted cumin seeds (page 13)

⅛ teaspoon cayenne pepper

½ teaspoon salt

¼ teaspoon garam masala (page 13)

2 teaspoons tomato purée

150 ml (¼ pint) chicken stock

6-8 hard-boiled eggs, peeled and cut crosswise into halves

1 tablespoon finely chopped fresh coriander or parsley, to garnish

1.   Heat the oil over a medium heat in a large, preferably non-stick, frying pan. When it is hot, put in the onion. Stir and fry the onion for about 3 minutes or until the pieces are browned at the edges. Put in the ginger and chilli. Stir and fry for 1 minute. Now put in the cream, lemon juice, ground roasted cumin, cayenne, salt, garam masala, tomato purée and chicken stock. Stir to mix thoroughly and bring to a simmer.

2.   Put all the egg halves into the sauce in a single layer, cut side up. Spoon the sauce over them. Cook over a medium heat for about 5 minutes, spooning the sauce frequently over the eggs as you do so. By this time the sauce will have become fairly thick. Put the egg halves carefully into a serving dish, cut side up, and pour the sauce over them. Garnish with the fresh coriander, sprinkling it lightly on the top.

From the left: Hard boiled eggs in a spicy cream sauce; Paratha (page 98)

Fisherman on Dal Lake, Srinagar, Kashmir
Inset: Fish drying, Bombay

FISH

THERE IS nothing quite like good fresh fish. It is light, cooks fast, and may be prepared simply and elegantly at the same time. Needless to say, the types of fish available in Indian rivers, lakes and seas are different from the ones found in the colder British waters. What used to be one of the common seafoods, fresh uncooked prawns, seems to have disappeared entirely from markets in Britain. I am hard put to understand why, since they can be found all over France, just a few miles away.

What I have done for this chapter is to work out Indian-style recipes for the fish that are commonly available in Britain. The prawns I have used are the cooked, packed frozen ones that are found in supermarkets or freezer centres and fishmongers. Just look for the largest and best varieties that you can find.

Indians eat a fair amount of breaded, fried fish. I have used plaice for this as it is similar to our pomfret, at least in general shape. Our mackerel has a plumper form but is very similar in taste. So I have used it for a west coast recipe that calls for a fresh coriander and lemon marinade. We have no cod, halibut or haddock in India but the textures of some of our river fish are similar. I have used them in Indian-style recipes in which they are cooked with tomatoes or yogurt or cauliflower.

I have even included a recipe for mussels. This is a Goan recipe, one of the few in this book that uses fresh coconut. It is an exquisite dish that can be made either with cockles or mussels.

I need hardly repeat that if you are buying fresh fish, make sure that it *is* fresh. The gills should be bright red, the eyes clear, the skin shiny, and the body firm and taut. The fish should not have a pronounced fishy odour.

Goan-style mussels

Thisra

ALTHOUGH EATEN with rice in Goa, I love to serve these mussels by themselves as a first course.

PREPARATION TIME: 40 minutes
COOKING TIME: 14-18 minutes

Serves 6	*1½-2 fresh hot green chillies, sliced into thin rounds*
30-36 mussels	
1 × 2.5 cm (1 inch) cube of fresh ginger, peeled and coarsely chopped	*½ teaspoon ground turmeric*
	2 teaspoons ground cumin
8 garlic cloves, peeled	*½ fresh coconut, finely grated (page 12)*
350 ml (12 fl oz) water	*½ teaspoon salt*
4 tablespoons vegetable oil	
175-200 g (6-7 oz) onions, peeled and chopped	

Clockwise from the left: Goan-style mussels;
Prawns with courgettes; Plain long-grain rice (page 107)   66

1.   Wash the mussels well, removing any beards. Discard any that remain open when tapped, any broken ones and any that float.
2.   Put the ginger and garlic into the container of an electric blender or food processor. Add 120 ml (4 fl oz) of the water and blend until fairly smooth.
3.   Heat the oil in a large saucepan over a medium flame. When it is hot, put in the onions and fry them until they turn trans-lucent. Now put in the paste from the blender, the green chillies, turmeric and cumin. Stir and fry for 1 minute. Add the coconut, salt and the remaining water. Bring to a boil. (This can be done several hours ahead of time.)
4.   Add the mussels. Mix well and bring to a boil. Cover tightly. Lower the heat slightly and let mussels steam for 6-10 minutes or until they open. Discard any which do not open. Serve immediately.

Prawns with courgettes

Jhinga aur ghia

WE DO NOT have courgettes in India but we do have a variety of similar squashes which are often cooked with prawns and other seafood. Here is one such combination. I prefer to use relatively small courgettes that weigh about 100 g (4 oz) each. If you can only get larger ones, just cut them appropriately so that each piece is just a little larger than a prawn.
I like to serve these prawns with Spiced basmati rice (page 106) or Plain long-grain rice (page 107) and Red split lentils with cumin seed (page 90).

PREPARATION TIME: 30 minutes, plus standing
COOKING TIME: 15 minutes

Serves 4
350 g (12 oz) courgettes (see above)
1 ¼ teaspoons salt
5 tablespoons vegetable oil
6 garlic cloves, peeled and very finely chopped
75 g (3 oz) finely chopped fresh coriander
1 fresh hot green chilli, finely chopped
½ teaspoon ground turmeric
1 ½ teaspoons ground cumin
¼ teaspoon cayenne
3 small canned tomatoes, finely chopped, plus 120 ml (4 fl oz) of their liquid
1 teaspoon very finely grated fresh ginger
1 tablespoon lemon juice
350 g (12 oz) good quality peeled prawns, defrosted if frozen, and patted dry

1.   Scrub the courgettes and trim them. Now cut them in 4 slices lengthwise, then cut each slice, lengthwise, into 4 long strips and cut the strips into thirds, crosswise. Put the courgettes in a bowl. Sprinkle ¼ teaspoon salt over the pieces. Toss to mix and set aside for 30-40 minutes. Drain and pat dry.
2.   Heat the oil in a wide saucepan or a frying pan over a medium-high flame. When it is hot, put in the chopped garlic. Stir and fry until the garlic turns a medium brown colour. Put in the courgettes, fresh coriander, green chilli, turmeric, cumin, cayenne, the tomatoes and their liquid, ginger, lemon juice and the remaining 1 teaspoon salt. Stir to mix and bring to a simmer. Add the prawns and stir them in. Cover, turn the heat to low and simmer for 3 minutes.
3.   Remove the lid, turn the heat to medium and boil away the excess liquid, if there is any, so that you are left with a thick sauce.

Prawns in a sauce

Rasedar jhinga

I LIKE TO SERVE these prawns with Plain basmati rice (page 107), Cauliflower with potatoes (page 83) and Tomato, onion and green coriander relish (page 124).

PREPARATION TIME: 30 minutes
COOKING TIME: 15 minutes

Serves 4

75 g (3 oz) onion, peeled and coarsely chopped

5 garlic cloves, peeled

1 × 2.5 cm (1 inch) cube of fresh ginger, peeled and coarsely chopped

3 tablespoons water, plus 300 ml (½ pint)

4 tablespoons vegetable oil

2.5 cm (1 inch) piece of cinnamon stick

6 cardamom pods

2 bay leaves

2 teaspoons ground cumin

1 teaspoon ground coriander

175 g (6 oz) tomatoes, peeled (page 18) and very finely chopped

5 tablespoons plain yogurt

½ teaspoon ground turmeric

¼-½ teaspoon cayenne pepper

about ¾ teaspoon salt

350 g (12 oz) good quality peeled prawns

¼ teaspoon garam masala (page 13)

2 tablespoons finely chopped fresh coriander

1. Put the onion, garlic, ginger and 3 tablespoons of water into the container of an electric blender or food processor and blend until you have a paste.
2. Heat the oil in a 20-23 cm (8-9 inch) wide saucepan over a medium-high flame. When hot, put in the cinnamon, cardamom and bay leaves. Stir for 3-4 seconds. Now put in the paste from the blender. Stir and fry for about 5 minutes or until the paste turns a light brown colour. Add the ground cumin and

Clockwise from top left: Tomato, onion and green coriander relish (page 124); Plain basmati rice (page 107); Prawns in a sauce; Halibut with cauliflower

coriander. Stir and fry for 30 seconds. Put in the tomatoes. Stir and keep frying until the paste has a nice reddish-brown look to it.

3.   Now put in 1 tablespoon of the yogurt. Stir and fry for 10-15 seconds or until it is incorporated into the sauce. Add all the yogurt this way, 1 tablespoon at a time. Put in the turmeric and cayenne and stir for 1 minute.

4.   Now put in 300 ml (½ pint) of water, the salt and the prawns. Stir to mix and bring to a boil over a medium-high flame. Stir and cook over this medium-high flame for about 5 minutes or until you have a good thick sauce. Do not overcook the prawns. Sprinkle the garam masala over the top and mix. Serve garnished with fresh coriander.

5.   The large whole spices are not meant to be eaten.

_H_alibut with cauliflower

Macchi aur phool gobi

ALL YOU NEED to serve with this dish is some rice and a relish.

PREPARATION TIME: 40 minutes, plus marinating
COOKING TIME: 20 minutes

Serves 4-6
1 × 2.5 cm (1 inch) thick halibut steak, total weight about 1 kg (2 lb)
1½ teaspoons ground cumin
1½ teaspoons ground coriander
½ teaspoon ground turmeric
about ½ teaspoon cayenne pepper
1½ teaspoons salt
100 g (4 oz) onion, peeled and coarsely chopped
2 × 2.5 cm (1 inch) cubes of fresh ginger, peeled and coarsely chopped
1-2 fresh hot green chillies, roughly cut into 3-4 pieces each
3 tablespoons water, plus 450 ml (¾ pint)
7 tablespoons vegetable oil
350 g (12 oz) cauliflower florets
freshly ground black pepper
6 tablespoons plain yogurt

1.   Have the fishmonger remove the bone and cut the halibut into pieces about 5 × 4 × 2.5 cm (2 × 1½ × 1 inch). Leave the skin on.

2.   Put the fish pieces into a bowl. Sprinkle ½ teaspoon each of the cumin and coriander, ¼ teaspoon each of the turmeric and cayenne and ½ teaspoon of the salt over them. Toss to mix evenly. Set aside for ½-1 hour.

3.   Put the onion, ginger, green chillies and 3 tablespoons of water into the container of an electric blender. Blend until you have a paste.

4.   Heat 6 tablespoons of the oil in a large deep frying pan over a medium flame. When it is hot, put in the cauliflower florets. Stir and fry them until they are very lightly browned. Remove with a slotted spoon and set aside in a bowl. Sprinkle ¼ teaspoon salt and some black pepper over the cauliflower. Toss to mix.

5.   Put the fish pieces into the same pan in a single layer and brown lightly on both sides. Do not let the fish cook through. Remove the fish pieces carefully and keep them on a plate.

6.   Add the remaining oil to the pan and heat on a medium-high flame. When it is hot, put in the paste from the blender. Stir and fry until it turns light brown. Now add the remaining cumin, coriander, cayenne, and salt. Stir and fry for 1 minute. Put in 1 tablespoon of the yogurt. Stir and fry it for about 30 seconds or until it is incorporated into the paste. Add all the yogurt this way, 1 tablespoon at a time. Now pour in the remaining water, stir and bring to a simmer. Simmer 2 minutes. Gently put in the fish pieces and the cauliflower. Cover partially and cook on a medium heat for 5 minutes or until the fish is cooked and the cauliflower is tender. Spoon the sauce over the fish and vegetables several times during this period.

Cod steaks in a spicy tomato sauce

Timatar wali macchi

I LIKE TO SERVE this with Rice with peas (page 109) and a spinach dish.

PREPARATION TIME: 10 minutes, plus standing
COOKING TIME: 40 minutes   OVEN: 180°C, 350°F, Gas Mark 4

Serves 4

4 cod steaks, total weight about 1 kg (2 lb)

1 ¼ teaspoons salt

½ teaspoon cayenne pepper

¼ teaspoon ground turmeric

9 tablespoons vegetable oil

1 teaspoon fennel seeds

1 teaspoon black mustard seeds

175 g (6 oz) onions, peeled and finely chopped

2 garlic cloves, peeled and finely chopped

2 teaspoons ground cumin

1 × 400 g (14 oz) can tomatoes, chopped

½ teaspoon ground, roasted cumin seeds (page 13), optional

¼ teaspoon garam masala (page 13)

1.   Pat the fish steaks dry with paper towels. Rub on both sides with ¼ teaspoon of the salt, ¼ teaspoon of the cayenne and ¼ teaspoon turmeric. Set aside for 30 minutes.

2.   Heat 4 tablespoons of the oil in a pan over a medium heat. When it is hot, put in the fennel and mustard seeds. As soon as the mustard seeds begin to pop (this takes just a few seconds), put in the onions and garlic. Stir and fry until the onions turn slightly brown. Now put in the cumin, 1 teaspoon salt and ¼ teaspoon cayenne. Stir once and put in the tomatoes and their liquid, the roasted cumin, and garam masala. Bring to a boil. Cover, turn the heat to low and simmer gently for 15 minutes.

3.   Put the remaining oil in a large frying pan and heat it over a medium-high flame. When it is hot, put in the fish steaks and brown them on both sides. Do not cook the fish through. Transfer the fish to a baking dish. Pour the sauce over and bake, uncovered, for 15 minutes or until the fish is done.

Grilled mackerel with lemon and fresh coriander

Hare masale wali macchi

INDIAN MACKEREL seems to me to be much plumper than their English counterparts. Goan fishermen roast them right on the beach over smouldering rice straw. The blackened skin is then peeled away and the pristine skinless fish served with a simple vinegar dressing. A good fresh mackerel needs nothing more. Further up the same coast, in large cities like Bombay, the fish is marinated in a dressing of lemon juice and fresh coriander and then fried or grilled. Here is the Bombay recipe. I often serve it with Mushroom pullao (page 110) and Cabbage with peas (page 80).

PREPARATION TIME: 15 minutes, plus marinating   COOKING TIME: about 10 minutes

Clockwise from top left; Cod steaks in a spicy tomato sauce; Rice with peas (page 109); Grilled mackerel with lemon and fresh coriander

Serves 2
2 medium mackerel, total weight about 750 g (1½ lb), cleaned
3 tablespoons very finely chopped fresh coriander
½-1 fresh, hot green chilli, finely chopped
1 tablespoon lemon juice
½ teaspoon salt
freshly ground black pepper
50 g (2 oz) unsalted butter, cut into pats

1. Cut the heads off the mackerel. Using a sharp knife, split the mackerel all the way down the stomach, and then lay them out flat, skin side up, on a firm surface.

2. Now bone the fish this way. Press down firmly with the heel of your hand all along the backbone. This should loosen the bone from the flesh somewhat. Now turn the fish over so the skin side is down. Work your fingers (or else use a knife) under the bones to prise them away from the flesh. Cut two to three shallow diagonal slashes on the skin side of each fish.

3. Combine the fresh coriander, chilli, lemon juice, salt and black pepper in a bowl. Mix well. Rub this mixture all over the fish. Set aside for 45 minutes.

4. Put the fish, skin side up, in the grill pan, with the rack removed and dot with half the butter. Cook, under a preheated grill, 10 cm (4 inches) away from the flame, for about 5 minutes. Turn the fish over, dot with the remaining butter and grill for 4 minutes or until golden brown.

*H*addock baked in a yogurt sauce

Dahi wali macchi

THIS IS ONE of my favourite fish dishes and it is so easy to put together. All you have to do is combine the ingredients in a baking dish and bake for about 30 minutes. You do have to boil down the sauce later but that takes just an additional 5 minutes. I like to serve this dish with Mushroom pullao (page 110) or Plain long-grain rice (page 107) and Frozen spinach with potatoes (page 85). You may also refrigerate this dish overnight and serve it cold with a green salad. This is not very traditional but we love it that way.

PREPARATION TIME: 20 minutes
COOKING TIME: 35 minutes
OVEN: 190°C, 375°F, Gas Mark 5

Serves 4-6
175 g (6 oz) onions, peeled
1 kg (2 lb) fresh haddock fillets, 2.5 cm (1 inch) thick
450 ml (¾ pint) plain yogurt
2 tablespoons lemon juice
1 teaspoon sugar
1½ teaspoons salt
¼ teaspoon coarsely ground black pepper
2 teaspoons ground cumin
2 tablespoons ground coriander
¼ teaspoon garam masala (page 13)
½-¾ teaspoon cayenne pepper
1 teaspoon peeled and finely grated fresh ginger
3 tablespoons vegetable oil
40 g (1½ oz) cold unsalted butter, cut into small pieces

1. Cut the onions into 3 mm (⅛ inch) thick slices and line a large baking dish with them. (The dish should be large enough to hold the fish in a single layer. It need not be more than 3 cm (1½ inches) deep.) Cut the fish fillets, crosswise, into 7.5 cm (3 inch) long segments and lay them over the onions.
2. Put the yogurt into a bowl. Beat it lightly. Add the lemon juice, sugar, salt, black pepper, cumin, coriander, garam masala, cayenne and ginger. Mix well. Add the oil and mix again. Pour this sauce over the fish, mak-ing sure that some of it goes under the pieces as well. Cover (with aluminium foil, if necessary) and bake on the top shelf of a preheated oven for 30 minutes or until the fish is just done.
3. Carefully pour all the liquid from the baking dish into a small saucepan. (Keep the fish covered and warm.) The sauce will look thin and 'separated'. Bring it to a boil. Boil rapidly until there is about 350 ml (12 fl oz) of sauce left. Take the saucepan off the heat. Put in the pieces of butter and beat them in with a fork. As soon as the butter has melted, pour the sauce over the fish and serve.

*F*ried plaice fillets

Tali hui macchi

THIS IS ONE of the simpler fish dishes served in many parts of India, with each area using its own local fish. The breading is, of course, a Western influence. Wedges of lemon or some tomato ketchup may be served on the side.

PREPARATION TIME: 25 minutes, plus marinating
COOKING TIME: about 15 minutes

Serves 4

750 g (1 ½ lb) plaice fillets, dark skin removed

¾ teaspoon salt

freshly ground black pepper

1 ½ teaspoons ground cumin

½ teaspoon ground turmeric

½ teaspoon cayenne pepper

2 tablespoons very finely chopped fresh coriander or parsley

2 eggs (size 1)

4 teaspoons water

175 g (6 oz) fresh breadcrumbs

vegetable oil for shallow frying

1. Cut the fish fillets crosswise and at a slight diagonal into 2 cm (¾ inch) wide strips. Lay the strips on a plate and sprinkle them on both sides with the salt, pepper, cumin, turmeric, cayenne and fresh coriander. Pat down the spices so they adhere to the fish. Set aside for 15 minutes.

2. Break the eggs into a bowl. Add 4 teaspoons water and beat lightly. Spread the breadcrumbs out on a plate. Dip the fish pieces first in the egg and then in the crumbs to coat them evenly.

3. Put a layer of oil, 1 cm (½ inch) deep, in a large frying pan and heat over a medium flame. When it is hot, put in as many pieces of fish as the pan will hold easily. Fry for 2-3 minutes on each side or until golden brown. Drain on paper towels. Fry all the fish strips in this way and serve hot.

Clockwise from top left: Haddock baked in a yogurt sauce with Plain long-grain rice (page 107); Fried plaice fillets; Frozen spinach with potatoes (page 85)

The Lake Palace Hotel, Udaipur
Inset: Floating vegetable market, Dal Lake, Kashmir

VEGETABLES

I LOVE ALL vegetables — from shiny purple aubergines that can be fried very simply with a light dusting of turmeric and cayenne to the humble potato which, in India, is cooked in at least a thousand different ways.

As many Indians are vegetarians, we have, over the years, worked out a great variety of ways to cook our everyday vegetables such as cabbages, green beans, beetroots and carrots. Sometimes the vegetables are cut into shreds or slices and quickly stir-fried with whole spices such as cumin and mustard seeds. These are referred to as 'dry' vegetables and rarely have even the glimmer of a sauce. At other times we may cook root vegetables in a thick ginger-garlic sauce or with tomatoes. Such dishes are referred to as 'wet' dishes because of the sauce. They are generally served in small, individual bowls. Both 'dry' and 'wet' dishes may be served with rice or Indian breads.

For those of you who are vegetarians — or want to cut down on your meat intake — you can make perfectly balanced meals by picking two or three vegetables from this chapter and then adding a pulse dish, a rice or bread and a yogurt relish.

Fried aubergine slices

Tala hua baigan

THIS IS ONE of the simplest ways of cooking aubergines in India. Ideally, the frying should be done at the very last minute and the melt-in-the mouth slices served as soon as they come out of the hot oil. Sometimes I arrange these slices, like petals, around a roast leg of lamb. They can, of course, be served with any Indian meal.

Leftover aubergine slices, if there are any, may be heated together with any leftover Indian-style meat the following day. The combination makes for a new dish and is very good.

PREPARATION TIME: 10 minutes
COOKING TIME: about 10-15 minutes

Serves 4-6
500 g (1¼ lb) aubergines
about 1 teaspoon salt
½ teaspoon ground turmeric
⅛-½ teaspoon ground cayenne pepper
freshly ground black pepper
vegetable oil for shallow frying
6-8 lemon wedges

1. Cut the aubergines into quarters, lengthwise, and then cut them, crosswise, into 1 cm (½ inch) thick chunks.
2. Mix the salt, turmeric, cayenne and black pepper in a small bowl. Sprinkle over the aubergines and mix well.
3. Heat about 1 cm (½ inch) of oil in a 20-23 cm (8-9 inch) frying pan over a medium flame. When it is hot, put in as many aubergine slices as the pan will hold in a single layer. Fry until reddish-gold on one side. Turn the slices and fry them on the other side. Remove the slices with a slotted spoon and spread them out on a plate lined with paper towels. Do a second batch, adding more oil, if you need to.
4. Serve with lemon wedges.

From the left: Fried aubergine slices; The Lake Palace Hotel's aubergine cooked in the pickling style

The Lake Palace Hotel's aubergine cooked in the pickling style

Baigan achari

RIGHT IN THE CENTRE of a lake in the formerly royal city of Udaipur is a summer palace, now converted, as most Indian palaces seem fated to be, into a spectacular hotel. This recipe comes from its master chef, Shankerlal, and in its finished effect is not unlike a spicy ratatouille. It is an exquisite dish. While *kalonji* – black onion seeds – do give this dish its special 'pickled' taste, you may use whole cumin seeds instead.

I love to eat this dish with a hearty lamb stew, such as *Rogan josh* (page 30) and a bread. If you do not feel like an all-Indian meal, you could serve it with roast lamb and plain rice. I think it also tastes excellent cold. I often dole out individual portions on lettuce leaves and serve them as a first course. Sometimes I serve this dish for lunch with cold chicken, cold lamb or sliced ham.

PREPARATION TIME: about 20 minutes, plus draining
COOKING TIME: about 35-45 minutes

Serves 6

1 × 2.5 cm (1 inch) cube of fresh ginger, peeled and coarsely chopped

6 large garlic cloves, peeled

3 tablespoons water

750 g (1 ½ lb) aubergines

475 ml (16 fl oz) vegetable oil

1 teaspoon fennel seeds

½ teaspoon kalonji or cumin seeds

350 g (12 oz) tomatoes, peeled (page 18) and finely chopped

1 tablespoon ground coriander

¼ teaspoon ground turmeric

about ⅓ teaspoon cayenne pepper

about 1 ¼ teaspoon salt

1.   Put the ginger and garlic into the container of an electric blender. Add the water and blend until fairly smooth.

2.   Cut the aubergines into slices or wedges about 2 cm (¾ inch) thick and about 4-5 cm (1½-2 inches) long.

3.   Set a sieve over a bowl.

4.   Heat 120 ml (4 fl oz) of the oil in a large deep frying pan or saucepan over a medium-high flame. When it is hot, put in as many aubergine slices as the pan will hold in a single layer. Let them turn a reddish-brown colour. Turn them over and brown the other side. Remove the slices and put them in the sieve. Add another 120 ml (4 fl oz) of oil to the frying pan and heat it. Brown a second batch of aubergine slices, just as you did the first. You will probably need to do three batches, adding fresh oil to the frying pan each time.

5.   (You may now let the aubergines drain for about 1 hour or you may proceed with the next step. The idea is to get rid of some of the oil that aubergines absorb so easily. You will achieve this either way, though I think it helps slightly to get rid of the oil at the earlier stage.)

6.   Put the remaining oil in the frying pan and heat it over a medium flame. When it is hot, put in the fennel seeds and *kalonji* or cumin seeds. As soon as the fennel seeds turn a few shades darker (this takes just a few seconds) put in the chopped tomato, the ginger-garlic mixture, coriander, turmeric, cayenne and salt. Stir and cook for 5-6 minutes. Turn the heat up slightly and continue to stir and cook until the spice mixture gets thick and pastelike.

7.   Now put in the fried aubergine slices and mix gently. Cook on a medium-low heat for about 5 minutes, stirring very gently as you do so. Cover the pan, turn the heat to very low and cook for another 5-10 minutes if you think it is necessary.

8.   Oil will have collected at the bottom of the frying pan. Use a slotted spoon to lift the aubergine out of this oil when you serve.

9.   You could also serve this dish cold, almost as if it were a salad. In that case, store it with all its oil in the refrigerator. Take it out of the oil only when you serve.

Spicy green beans

Masaledar sem

THESE GREEN BEANS may, of course, be served with an Indian dinner. But they could perk up a simple meal of roast chicken, pork chops or meat loaf as well. They are tart and hot and would complement the plainest of everyday foods with their zesty blend of flavours. Another good thing about them – they may be made ahead of time and reheated.

PREPARATION TIME: 25 minutes
COOKING TIME: about 15 minutes

Serves 6
750 g (1 ½ lb) fresh green French beans
1 × 4 cm × 2.5 cm (1 ½ × 1 inch) piece of fresh ginger, peeled and chopped
10 garlic cloves, peeled
350 ml (12 fl oz) water
5 tablespoons vegetable oil
2 teaspoons cumin seeds
1 dried hot red chilli, lightly crushed in a mortar
2 teaspoons ground coriander
225 g (8 oz) tomatoes, peeled (page 18) and finely chopped
about 1 ¼ teaspoons salt
3 tablespoons lemon juice – or to taste
1 teaspoon ground, roasted cumin seeds (page 13)
freshly ground black pepper

1.   Trim the green beans and cut them, crosswise, into small pieces. Put the ginger and garlic into the container of an electric blender or food processor. Add 120 ml (4 fl oz) of the water and blend until fairly smooth.

2.   Heat the oil in a wide, heavy saucepan over a medium flame. When it is hot, put in the cumin seeds. Five seconds later, put in the crushed chilli. As soon as it darkens, pour in the ginger-garlic paste. Stir and cook for about 1 minute. Put in the coriander. Stir a few times.

3.   Now put in the chopped tomatoes. Stir and cook for about 2 minutes, mashing up the tomato pieces with the back of a slotted spoon as you do so. Put in the beans, salt and the remaining water. Bring to a simmer. Cover, turn the heat to low and cook for about 8-10 minutes or until the beans are tender.

4.   Remove the lid. Add the lemon juice, roasted cumin and a generous amount of freshly ground pepper. Turn up the heat and boil away all the liquid, stirring the beans gently as you do so.

Gujerati-style green beans

Gujerati sem

HERE IS A VERY SIMPLE, yet delicious way to cook green beans. This dish goes well both with Indian meals and with grilled and roasted meats (I like it with sausages). Gujeratis often cook green vegetables with a little baking soda to preserve their bright colour. I am told that this kills the vitamins. So I blanch the beans and rinse them out quickly under cold running water instead. This works equally well. I generally do the blanching and rinsing quite a bit ahead of time and do the final cooking just before we sit down to eat.

If you do not want the beans to be hot, either do without the red chilli or else discard all its seeds and use just the skin for flavour.

PREPARATION TIME: 10 minutes   COOKING TIME: about 15 minutes

Serves 4

450 g (1 lb) fresh green French beans

4 tablespoons vegetable oil

1 tablespoon black mustard seeds

4 garlic cloves, peeled and very finely chopped

½-1 hot dried red chilli, coarsely crushed in a mortar

1 teaspoon salt

½ teaspoon sugar

freshly ground black pepper

1.   Trim the beans and cut them into 2.5 cm (1 inch) lengths. Blanch the beans by dropping them into a pot of boiling water and boiling rapidly for 3-4 minutes or until they are just tender. Drain immediately in a colander and rinse them under cold running water. Set on one side.

2.   Heat the oil in a large frying pan over a medium flame. When it is hot, put in the mustard seeds. As soon as the mustard seeds begin to pop, put in the garlic. Stir the garlic pieces around until they turn light brown. Put in the crushed red chilli and stir for a few seconds. Put in the green beans, salt and sugar. Stir to mix. Turn the heat to medium-low. Stir and cook the beans for 7-8 minutes or until they have absorbed the flavour of the spices. Add the black pepper, mix and serve.

Clockwise from top left: Spicy green beans; Gujerati-style green beans; Carrots, peas and potatoes flavoured with cumin (page 80)

Carrots, peas and potatoes flavoured with cumin

Pictured on
page 79

Gajar, matar, aur aloo ki bhaji

HERE IS a simple, quick-cooking dish. Ideally, it should be made in an Indian *karhai* but if you do not have one, a large frying pan or sauté pan will do. The vegetables are cooked in a Bengali style but could easily accompany a roast chicken or grilled sausages.

PREPARATION TIME: 20 minutes
COOKING TIME: 14 minutes

Serves 6
175 g (6 oz) carrots
175 g (6 oz) potatoes, boiled, drained and cooled
175 g (6 oz) onions
1 spring onion
3 tablespoons mustard oil (another vegetable oil may be substituted)
1 ½ teaspoons whole cumin seeds
2 whole dried hot red chillies
175 g (6 oz) shelled peas
about 1 teaspoon salt
¼ teaspoon sugar

1.   Peel the carrots and cut them first into 1 cm (½ inch) thick diagonal slices and then into 1 cm (½ inch) pieces.

2.   Peel the potatoes and cut them into 1 cm (½ inch) dice. Peel the onions and chop them coarsely. Cut the spring onion into very, very thin slices, all the way to the end of its green section.

3.   Heat the oil in a large frying pan over a medium flame. When it is hot, put in the cumin seeds. Let them sizzle for 3-4 seconds. Now put in the whole chillies and stir them about for 3-4 seconds.

4.   Put in the chopped onion. Stir and cook for 5 minutes or until the onion pieces turn translucent. Put in the carrots and peas. Stir them about for 1 minute. Cover, turn the heat to low, and cook for about 5 minutes or until the vegetables are tender.

5.   Remove the lid and turn the heat up slightly. Add the potatoes, salt and sugar. Stir and cook for another 2-3 minutes. Add the spring onion. Stir and cook for 30 seconds.

6.   Remove the whole chillies before serving this dish.

Cabbage with peas

Bund gobi aur matar

HERE IS A SIMPLE cabbage dish that you could serve just as easily with grilled pork chops as with an Indian meal.

PREPARATION TIME: 10 minutes   COOKING TIME: 8-9 minutes

Serves 4	¼ teaspoon cayenne pepper
450-500 g (1-1¼lb) green cabbage	1 fresh hot green chilli, very finely chopped
150 g (5 oz) frozen peas	¾ teaspoon salt
5 tablespoons vegetable oil	¾ teaspoon sugar
2 teaspoons cumin seeds	¼ teaspoon garam masala (page 13)
2 bay leaves	
¼ teaspoon ground turmeric	

1.　　Core the cabbage and cut it into very fine, long shreds. Put the peas into a strainer and hold them under warm, running water until they separate.

2.　　Heat the oil in a wide saucepan over a medium-high flame. When it is hot, put in the cumin seeds and bay leaves. As soon as the bay leaves begin to take on colour — this takes just a few seconds — put in the cabbage and peas and stir them about for 30 seconds. Add the turmeric and cayenne. Stir to mix. Cover, turn the heat to low and cook for 5 minutes or until the vegetables are just tender. Add the green chilli, salt and sugar. Stir to mix. Cover and cook on a low heat for another 2-3 minutes. Remove the lid and sprinkle in the garam masala. Stir gently to mix.

3.　　Remove the bay leaves before serving.

Gujerati-style cabbage with carrots

Sambhara

THIS everyday vegetable dish may be served equally well with pork chops as with an Indian meal.

PREPARATION TIME: 20 minutes　　COOKING TIME: about 7 minutes

Serves 4-6
350 g (12 oz) green English cabbage
350 g (12 oz) carrots
½-1 fresh hot green chilli
4 tablespoons vegetable oil
pinch of ground asafetida (optional)
1 tablespoon black mustard seeds
1 hot dried red chilli
about 1¼ teaspoons salt
½ teaspoon sugar
4 heaped tablespoons chopped fresh coriander
1 tablespoon lemon juice

1.　　Core the cabbage and cut it into long shreds. Peel and grate the carrots coarsely. Cut the green chilli into thin, long strips.

2.　　Heat the oil in a wide flameproof casserole over a medium-high flame. When it is hot, put in the asafetida if using. One second later, put in the mustard seeds. As soon as the mustard seeds begin to pop (this takes just a few seconds), put in the dried red chilli. Stir once. The chilli should turn dark red in seconds.

3.　　Now put in the cabbage, carrots and green chilli. Turn the heat down to medium and stir the vegetables around for 30 seconds. Add the salt, sugar and fresh coriander. Stir and cook for another 5 minutes or until the vegetables are just done and retain some of their crispness. Add the lemon juice and mix.

4.　　Remove the whole red chilli before serving to those unfamiliar with Indian foods.

From the top: Gujerati-style cabbage with carrots; Cabbage with peas

Cauliflower with onion and tomato

Phool gobi ki bhaji

A GOOD all-round vegetable dish that goes well with most Indian meat dishes.

PREPARATION TIME: 25 minutes, plus soaking
COOKING TIME: 10-15 minutes

Serves 6	1 teaspoon ground cumin
2 medium cauliflowers, total weight about 1 kg (2¼ lb) (you need about 750 g (1¾ lb) florets)	1 teaspoon ground coriander
	150-175 g (5-6 oz) tomatoes, peeled (page 18) and finely chopped
75 g (3 oz) onion, peeled and coarsely chopped	½ teaspoon ground turmeric
2 × 2.5 cm (1 inch) cubes of fresh ginger, peeled and coarsely chopped	⅛-½ teaspoon cayenne pepper
	½-1 fresh hot green chilli, finely chopped
7-8 tablespoons water	1 tablespoon lemon juice
5 tablespoons vegetable oil	1¾ teaspoons salt
6 garlic cloves, peeled and very finely chopped	¼ teaspoon garam masala (page 13)

From the left: Cauliflower with onion and
tomato; Cauliflower with potatoes

1.   Break up the cauliflowers into florets about 4 cm (1½ inches) across and 4-5 cm (1½-2 inches) long. Let them soak in a bowl of water for 30 minutes. Drain.

2.   Put the onion and ginger into the container of an electric blender with 4 tablespoons of water. Blend until you have a paste.

3.   Heat the oil in a 23-25 cm (9-10 inch) wide saucepan or deep frying pan over a medium-high flame. When it is hot, put in the garlic. Stir and fry until the pieces turn a medium-brown colour. Put in the cauliflower. Stir and fry for about 2 minutes or until the cauliflower pieces pick up a few brown spots. Remove the cauliflower with a slotted spoon and put it in a bowl.

4.   Put the onion-ginger mixture into the same pan. Stir and fry it for 1 minute. Now put in the cumin, coriander and tomato. Stir and fry this mixture until it turns a medium brown colour. If it starts to catch, turn the heat down slightly and sprinkle in 1 tablespoon of water. Then keep frying until you have the right colour. Add the turmeric, cayenne, green chilli, lemon juice and salt. Give a few good stirs and turn the heat to low.

5.   Now put in the cauliflower and any liquid remaining in the cauliflower bowl. Stir gently to mix. Add the remaining water, stir again and bring to a simmer. Cover and cook on a gentle heat, stirring now and then, for 5-10 minutes or until the cauliflower is just done. Remove the lid and sprinkle garam masala over the top. Stir to mix.

Cauliflower with potatoes

Phool gobi aur aloo ki bhaji

THIS IS the kind of comforting 'homey' dish that most North Indians enjoy. It has no sauce and is generally eaten with a bread. I like to serve *Shahi korma* (page 34) or Tandoori-style chicken (page 48) with it.

PREPARATION TIME: 15 minutes, plus soaking   COOKING TIME: about 35 minutes

Serves 4-6
225 g (8 oz) potatoes
1 medium cauliflower (you need 450 g (1 lb) of florets)
5 tablespoons vegetable oil
1 teaspoon cumin seeds
1 teaspoon ground cumin
½ teaspoon ground coriander
¼ teaspoon ground turmeric
¼ teaspoon cayenne pepper
½-1 fresh hot green chilli, very finely chopped
½ teaspoon ground roasted cumin seeds (page 13)
1 teaspoon salt
freshly ground black pepper

1.   Boil the potatoes in their jackets and allow them to cool completely. Peel the potatoes and cut them into 2 cm (¾ inch) dice.

2.   Break up the cauliflower into chunky florets, about 4 cm (1½ inches) across and about 4 cm (1½ inches) long. Soak the florets in a bowl of water for 30 minutes. Drain.

3.   Heat the oil in a large, preferably non-stick, frying pan over a medium flame. When it is hot, put in the cumin seeds. Let the seeds sizzle for 3-4 seconds. Now put in the cauliflower and stir it about for 2 minutes. Let the cauliflower brown in spots. Cover, turn the heat to low and simmer for about 4-6 minutes or until the cauliflower is almost done but still has a hint of crispness left.

4.   Put in the diced potatoes, ground cumin, coriander, turmeric, cayenne, green chilli, ground roasted cumin, salt and some black pepper. Stir gently to mix. Continue to cook uncovered on a low heat for another 3 minutes or until the potatoes are heated through. Stir gently as you do so.

Mushrooms and potatoes cooked with garlic and ginger

Rasedar khumbi aloo

THIS IS one of those 'home-style' dishes that you rarely find in Indian restaurants. It is a thick, earthy stew that used to be made only when slim, monsoon mushrooms made a brief, seasonal appearance. Now, even in Indian cities, you can buy cultivated white mushrooms all year round. Since these mushrooms come in a variety of sizes, you will have to use your own judgement about whether you should halve them, quarter them, or leave them whole. They should end up being about the same size as the diced potatoes.
You could serve this with Beef baked with yogurt and black pepper (page 27) and Gujerati carrot salad (page 123).

PREPARATION TIME: 25 minutes
COOKING TIME: 35 minutes

Serves 4-6

250-275 g (9-10 oz) potatoes

350 g (12 oz) mushrooms

1 × 2.5 cm (1 inch) cube of fresh ginger, peeled

6 large garlic cloves, peeled

3 tablespoons water, plus 250 ml (8 fl oz)

about 1 teaspoon salt

about ½ teaspoon ground turmeric

4 tablespoons vegetable oil

1 teaspoon cumin seeds

3 cardamom pods

275 g (10 oz) tomatoes, peeled (page 18) and finely chopped

1 teaspoon ground cumin

½ teaspoon ground coriander

about ¼ teaspoon cayenne pepper

¼ teaspoon garam masala (page 13)

1 tablespoon finely chopped fresh coriander, to garnish

1. Boil the potatoes in their jackets. Drain and peel them. Cut into 2.5 cm (1 inch) cubes.
2. Wipe the mushrooms with a damp cloth. Cut off the lower woody part of the stems. Now, depending upon their size, halve or quarter the mushrooms, or, if they are small, leave them whole. They should be about the size of the diced potatoes.

3. Put the ginger and garlic into the container of a food processor or electric blender along with the 3 tablespoons of water. Blend until you have a fine purée.
4. Put the diced potatoes into a bowl. Sprinkle about ¼ teaspoon salt and about ⅛ teaspoon of the turmeric over them. Toss to mix and set aside.
5. Heat the oil in a heavy, wide, preferably non-stick, pan over a medium flame. When it is hot, put in the potatoes. Stir and fry them until they are lightly browned on all sides. Remove the potato pieces with a slotted spoon and set them aside on a plate.
6. Put the whole cumin seeds and cardamom pods into the same pot. Stir them about for 3-4 seconds. Now put in the tomatoes, the ginger-garlic paste, the ground cumin and the ground coriander. Stir and fry until the paste becomes thick and the oil separates from it. Add ¼ teaspoon turmeric and the cayenne. Stir once or twice.
7. Put in the remaining water, the potatoes, mushrooms and ¾ teaspoon salt. Stir to mix and bring to a simmer. Cover, turn the heat to low and simmer for 5 minutes. Remove the lid and turn up the heat slightly. Cook, stirring gently, until you have a thick sauce. Sprinkle in the garam masala and stir to mix. Taste for salt and adjust if necessary.
8. Serve garnished with fresh coriander.
9. The whole cardamom pods are not meant to be eaten.

*F*rozen spinach with potatoes

Saag aloo

IN INDIA, we combine potatoes with almost every grain, meat, and vegetable. Here is one of my favourite recipes. It may be served with Red lamb or beef stew, *Rogan josh* (page 30) and an Indian bread or rice.

PREPARATION TIME: 20 minutes   COOKING TIME: 55 minutes

Serves 4-6

300 ml (½ pint) water, plus 2 tablespoons

500 g (1¼ lb) frozen leaf spinach

100 g (4 oz) onions, peeled

5 tablespoons vegetable oil

pinch of ground asafetida (optional)

2 teaspoons black mustard seeds

2 garlic cloves, peeled and finely chopped

500 g (1¼ lb) potatoes, peeled and cut roughly into 2-2.5 cm (¾-1 inch) cubes

¼ teaspoon cayenne pepper

1 teaspoon salt

1.   Bring 300 ml (½ pint) water to a boil in a saucepan. Put in the spinach, cover, and cook until it is just done. Drain in a colander and rinse under cold water. Press out most of the liquid in the leaves (you need not be too thorough) and then chop them coarsely.

2.   Cut the onions in half lengthwise, and then crosswise into very thin slices.

3.   Heat the oil in a heavy saucepan over a medium flame. When it is hot, put in the asafetida, if using, and then, 1 second later, the mustard seeds. As soon as the mustard seeds begin to pop (this takes just a few seconds) put in the onions and garlic. Stir and fry for 2 minutes. Put in the potatoes and cayenne. Stir and fry for a few minutes.

4.   Now put in the spinach, salt and 2 tablespoons water. Bring to a boil. Cover tightly, then turn the heat to very low and cook gently for 40 minutes or until the potatoes are tender. Stir a few times during the cooking period and make sure that there is always a little liquid in the saucepan.

Clockwise from the left: Mushrooms and potatoes cooked with garlic and ginger; Poori (page 101); Frozen spinach with potatoes; Gujerati carrot salad (page 123)

From the left: Turnips with fresh coriander and mint; Poppadum (page 130); Sweet and sour okra

Turnips with fresh coriander and mint

Rasedar shaljum

I HAVE ALWAYS had a fondness for turnips. The same, however, was not true for my three
children, until I finally won them over with this dish.
You could serve turnips with Lamb with onions (page 28) and rice or an Indian bread.

PREPARATION TIME: 20 minutes   COOKING TIME: 35 minutes

Serves 6	*½ teaspoon ground turmeric*
1 kg (2 lb) turnips	*¼-½ teaspoon cayenne pepper*
4 tablespoons vegetable oil	*450 ml (¾ pint) water*
350 g (12 oz) fresh tomatoes, peeled (page 18) or use canned tomatoes	*3 tablespoons very finely chopped fresh coriander*
1 × 2.5 cm (1 inch) cube of fresh ginger, peeled and grated to a pulp	*2 tablespoons very finely chopped fresh mint*
1 tablespoon ground coriander	*1½ teaspoons salt*

1.   Peel the turnips and cut them in half, lengthwise. Put the cut ends flat against your chopping board and cut them, lengthwise, into 1 cm (½ inch) thick slices.
2.   Heat the oil in a fairly wide pan over a medium-high flame. When it is hot, put in the tomatoes. Stir and fry for about 2 minutes.

Add the ginger, coriander, turmeric and cayenne. Stir and fry for another 2 minutes or until the sauce is thick and paste-like. Add the turnips, water, fresh coriander, mint and salt. Cover, leaving the lid very slightly open, and cook on a medium-low heat for 20 minutes. Stir a few times as the turnips cook.

3.   Now cover the saucepan tightly with a lid and cook on a low heat for another 10 minutes or until the turnips are tender. You should have a little thick sauce left at the bottom of your saucepan which can be served spooned over the turnips.

Sweet and sour okra

Kutchhi bhindi

HERE IS an absolutely wonderful way to cook okra. It tastes at its very best when made with young tender pods.

It may be served with Lamb with onions (page 28) and Mushroom pullao (page 110).

PREPARATION TIME: 15 minutes   COOKING TIME: 12 minutes

Serves 4-6
400 g (14 oz) fresh, tender okra (bhindi)
7 medium garlic cloves, peeled
1 whole dried hot red chilli (use half if you want it very mild)
7-8 tablespoons water
2 teaspoons ground cumin
1 teaspoon ground coriander
½ teaspoon ground turmeric
4 tablespoons vegetable oil
1 teaspoon cumin seeds
about 1 teaspoon salt
1 teaspoon sugar
about 4 teaspoons lemon juice

1.   Rinse the fresh okra and pat it dry. Trim the pods by cutting off the ends. The top is usually trimmed with a paring knife to leave a cone-shaped head, and a tiny piece is just snipped off the bottom. Cut the okra into 2 cm (¾ inch) lengths.

2.   Put the garlic and chilli into the container of an electric blender with 3 tablespoons of the water. Blend them together until you have a smooth paste.

3.   Empty the paste into a small bowl. Add the ground cumin, coriander and turmeric. Mix together thoroughly.

4.   Heat the oil in a 23 cm (9 inch) frying pan or sauté pan over a medium flame. When it is hot put in the cumin seeds. As soon as the cumin seeds begin to sizzle (this happens within a few seconds), turn the heat down a bit and pour in the spice mixture from the small bowl. Stir and fry for about 1 minute.

5.   Now put in the okra, salt, sugar, lemon juice and the remaining water. Stir to mix and bring to a gentle simmer. Cover tightly and cook on low heat for about 10 minutes or until the okra is tender. If your okra takes longer to cook, you might need a little more water.

Krishna painting Radha's toenails while two maids look on, Northern Indian painting, mid 19th century

Market place, Udaipur, Rajasthan

PULSES

PULSES — dried beans, split peas, and lentils — are a staple in India and help provide a large measure of the daily protein for families who eat meat rarely or are vegetarian.

But beans, by themselves, are an incomplete food and need to be complemented — at the same meal — with a grain (rice or bread) and a dairy product (such as yogurt or cheese). When nutritionists tell us today that this food combination has as much protein as a steak, I cannot help but think of the villagers in India whose basic diet for centuries has been *dals* (split peas) and rice or bread, washed down with a glass of buttermilk.

Sometimes pulses can be hard to digest. The same Indian forbears who worked out that a nutritionally balanced vegetarian meal contained pulses, grains, and dairy products, also knew — I do not know how — that certain seasonings made beans more digestible. Today pulses in India are almost always cooked with at least one of the following: ginger, asafetida and turmeric.

We have many different types of pulses in India. Some are left whole, others are split and sometimes skinned. It is the split peas that are called *dals*. The splitting helps to cook them much faster.

All pulses need to be picked over and washed as the packets often include small stones and husks. Whole beans should either be soaked in water overnight before they are cooked or else they can be boiled in water for 2 minutes and then left to soak in the same water for an hour. The cooking time for all pulses varies according to their freshness. The fresher they are, the faster they cook. When cooking split peas, Indians always leave the lid slightly open. This is because split peas create a lot of thick froth as they cook and this blocks up the normal escape routes for the steam. So the pot boils over, creating a mess on the cooker. Leaving the lid slightly open helps to avoid this.

Red split lentils (1)
Masoor dal

Whole green lentils (2)
Sabith hari dal

Moong dal (3)
Husked and split

Moong dal (4)
Split

(1) These round split lentils turn pale yellow during cooking and have a pleasant mild flavour. (2) Very similar to our unsplit, unskinned *masoor*, green lentils have the virtue of cooking quite fast. (3) and (4) Moong dal is perhaps the most popular North Indian dal. It is the dried version of the mung bean used to make bean sprouts for oriental cooking. The unhusked beans are green and the split ones are pale yellow.

Chana dal (5)

Yellow split peas (6)

Chick peas (7)
Chhole

Chana dal (5) are very like yellow split peas (6), but smaller, 'meatier' and sweeter. They are sold mainly by Indian grocers. Yellow split peas may be used instead in my recipes. The large heart-shaped chick pea (7) lends itself to being cooked as a spicy snack as well as being combined with meats and vegetables.

Red kidney beans (8)
Rajma

Black-eyed beans (9)
Lobhia

Aduki beans (10)
Ma

The large dark red kidney beans (8) are widely available. Greyish or beige ovals graced with a dark dot, the excellent black-eyed beans (9) have a slightly smoky flavour. The smaller red aduki beans (10) look like the children of red kidney beans. For some reason they are sold by their Japanese name in most shops and supermarkets.

Red split lentils with cumin seed

Masoor dal aur sabut zeera

THIS SALMON COLOURED split pea turns dull yellow when cooked. They are sold as Egyptian lentils in some Middle Eastern stores and are best served with a rice dish and almost any Indian meat and vegetable you like.

PREPARATION TIME: 10 minutes
COOKING TIME: about 1½ hours

Serves 4-6
200 g (7 oz) red split lentils (masoor dal), washed and drained
1 litre (1¾ pints) water
2 thin slices unpeeled ginger
½ teaspoon ground turmeric
1 teaspoon salt, or to taste
3 tablespoons ghee (page 16) or vegetable oil
pinch of ground asafetida (optional)
1 teaspoon cumin seeds
1 teaspoon ground coriander
¼ teaspoon cayenne pepper
2 tablespoons chopped fresh coriander

1. Combine the lentils and the water in a heavy saucepan. Bring to a simmer. Skim. Add the ginger and turmeric. Stir to mix. Cover, leaving the lid very slightly open, turn the heat to low, and simmer gently for 1 hour or until the lentils are tender. Stir every 5 minutes during the last 30 minutes to prevent sticking. Add the salt and stir to mix. Remove the ginger slices.
2. Heat the ghee in a small frying pan over a medium flame. When it is hot, put in the asafetida, if using. One second later, put in the cumin seeds. Let the seeds sizzle for a few seconds. Now put in the ground coriander and cayenne. Stir once and then quickly pour the contents of the pan into the saucepan with the lentils. Stir to mix.
3. Sprinkle over the fresh coriander.

From the left: Red split lentils with cumin seed; Whole green lentils with spinach and ginger

Whole green lentils with spinach and ginger

Sabut hari dal saag aur adrak ke sath

THIS VERY nourishing dish goes well with Beef baked with yogurt and black pepper (page 27).

PREPARATION TIME: 15 minutes   COOKING TIME: about 1½ hours

Serves 6

200 g (7 oz) green lentils, washed and drained

750 ml (1¼ pints) water

6 tablespoons vegetable oil

1-2 fresh hot green chillies, finely sliced

1 teaspoon very finely grated fresh ginger

8 well-packed tablespoons chopped fresh coriander

500 g (1¼ lb) fresh spinach, trimmed, washed and chopped

salt

freshly ground black pepper

2 tablespoons lemon juice, or to taste

1.   Put the lentils and the water into a heavy saucepan and bring to a boil. Cover, turn the heat to low and simmer gently for 1 hour.

2.   Over a medium flame, heat the oil in a saucepan large enough to hold the spinach. When it is hot, put in the chillies and the ginger. Stir and fry for 10 seconds. Add the fresh coriander and the spinach. Stir and cook until the spinach has wilted. Now put in the cooked lentils and 2 teaspoons salt. Stir to mix and bring to a simmer. Cover and cook very gently for 25 minutes. Add the black pepper and lemon juice, stir to mix, and cook uncovered for another 5 minutes. Check the seasoning and adjust if necessary.

Whole green lentils with garlic and onion

Sabut hari dal lassun aur pyaz ke sath

THIS IS a very simple — and flavourful — method of cooking the humble lentil. You could serve it with Goan-style hot and sour pork (page 42) or any other meat dish and some rice.

PREPARATION TIME: 10 minutes   COOKING TIME: about 1¼ hours

Serves 4-6
4 tablespoons vegetable oil
½ teaspoon cumin seeds
4 garlic cloves, peeled and finely chopped
75 g (3 oz) onion, peeled and chopped
200 g (7 oz) whole green lentils, washed and drained
750 ml (1¼ pints) water
1 teaspoon salt
⅛-¼ teaspoon cayenne pepper

1.   Heat the oil in a heavy saucepan over a medium flame. When it is hot, put in the cumin seeds. A few seconds later, put in the garlic. Stir and fry until the garlic pieces turn a medium brown colour. Now put in the onion. Stir and fry until the onion pieces begin to turn brown at the edges. Put in the lentils and the water. Bring to a boil. Cover, turn the heat to low and simmer for about 1 hour or until the lentils are tender. Add the salt and the cayenne. Stir to mix and simmer gently for another 5 minutes.

Small yellow split peas

Chana dal

OF ALL THE DALS, this one perhaps has the 'meatiest' taste. At its best, it also has a gentle sweetness. Chana dal is sold only by Indian grocers. If you cannot find it, substitute yellow split peas. You could serve this dal with rice and Chicken with tomatoes and garam masala (page 57).

PREPARATION TIME: 10 minutes   COOKING TIME: about 1¾ hours

Serves 4-6
225 g (8 oz) chana dal or yellow split peas, washed and drained
1.2 litres (2 pints) water
½ teaspoon ground turmeric
2 thin slices of unpeeled ginger
¾-1 teaspoon salt
¼ teaspoon garam masala (page 13)
3 tablespoons ghee (page 16)
½ teaspoon cumin seeds
1-2 garlic cloves, peeled and chopped
¼-½ teaspoon red chilli powder

1.   Put the dal into a heavy saucepan along with the water. Bring to a boil and skim. Add the turmeric and ginger. Cover, leaving the lid just very slightly open, turn the heat to low, and simmer gently for 1½ hours or until the dal is tender. Stir every 5 minutes or so during the last 30 minutes of cooking to prevent sticking. Add the salt and garam masala to the dal. Stir to mix.

2.   Heat the ghee in a small frying pan over a medium flame. When it is hot, put in the cumin seeds. A couple of seconds later, put in the garlic. Stir and fry until the garlic pieces are lightly browned. Put the chilli powder into the pan. Immediately, lift the pan off the heat and pour its entire contents into the saucepan with the dal. Stir to mix.

Dry moong dal

Sookhi moong dal

NOT ALL dals are cooked to be thin and soupy. Here the grains stand out, all plump and separate, and the dal has a fairly dry look. It is usually eaten not with rice but with breads and other meats and vegetables. I love to sprinkle some crisp browned onions over the top just before I serve it. Those unfamiliar with Indian foods should be warned that the whole chilli is very hot and not meant to be eaten — except by those who know what they are doing.

PREPARATION TIME: 10 minutes, plus soaking
COOKING TIME: 17 minutes

Serves 4-6	1 teaspoon ground coriander
200 g (7 oz) moong dal, washed and drained	1 teaspoon ground cumin
	1/4 teaspoon ground turmeric
1.2 litres (2 pints) water, plus 1 tablespoon	1/8 - 1/4 teaspoon cayenne pepper
	2 tablespoons vegetable oil
	about 1/2 teaspoon salt
	2 tablespoons ghee (page 16)
	1/2 teaspoon cumin seeds
	1 whole hot dried red chilli (optional)

1.   Put the dal into a bowl. Pour about 900 ml (1½ pints) of water over it and let it soak for 3 hours. Drain.

2.   Combine the coriander, cumin, turmeric, cayenne and 1 tablespoon of water.

3.   Heat the oil in a heavy pan over a medium flame. When it is hot, put in the spice mixture and stir once. Quickly put in the drained dal. Stir to mix. Add the salt and the remaining 250 ml (8 fl oz) water. Bring to a boil. Cover tightly, turn the heat to very low, and cook for 15 minutes. The dal grains should now be quite tender.

4.   Just before you sit down to eat, put the hot moong dal into a serving bowl. Heat the ghee in a small saucepan or a small frying pan. When it is very hot, put in the whole cumin seeds. Let them sizzle for a few seconds. Now put in the whole chilli and stir it about for 2-3 seconds — it should puff up and darken. Now pour the ghee and spices over the cooked dal. You may stir to mix or else leave the spices on the top as a kind of garnish.

5.   If you decide to use the fried onions, sprinkle these over the dal at the last minute.

From the top: Whole green lentils with garlic and onion; Small yellow split peas; Dry moong dal

93

Black-eyed beans with mushrooms

Lobhia aur khumbi

I LIKE THIS bean dish so much, I often find myself eating it up with a spoon, all by itself. At a meal, I serve it with *Rogan josh* (Red lamb or beef stew, page 30), or with Chicken in a fried onion sauce (page 53). Rice or Indian breads should be served on the side.

PREPARATION TIME: 25 minutes, plus 1 hour sitting
COOKING TIME: about 1-1¼ hours

Serves 6
225g (8 oz) dried black-eyed beans, picked over, washed and drained
1.2 litres (2 pints) water
225 g (8 oz) fresh mushrooms
6 tablespoons vegetable oil
1 teaspoon cumin seeds
2.5 cm (1 inch) piece of cinnamon stick
150 g (5 oz) onions, peeled and chopped
4 garlic cloves, peeled and very finely chopped
400 g (14 oz) tomatoes, peeled (page 18) and chopped
2 teaspoons ground coriander
1 teaspoon ground cumin
½ teaspoon ground turmeric
¼ teaspoon cayenne pepper
2 teaspoons salt
freshly ground black pepper
3 tablespoons chopped fresh coriander (or use fresh parsley)

1.   Put the beans and water into a heavy saucepan and bring to a boil. Cover, turn the heat to low and simmer gently for 2 minutes. Turn off the heat and let the pan sit, covered and undisturbed, for 1 hour.

2.   While the pan is resting, cut the mushrooms through their stems into 3 mm (⅛ inch) thick slices.

3.   Heat the oil in a frying pan over a medium-high flame. When it is hot, put in the cumin seeds and the cinnamon stick. Let them sizzle for 5-6 seconds. Now put in the onions and garlic. Stir and fry until the onion pieces

Clockwise from the top: Black-eyed beans with mushrooms; Red kidney beans; Plain basmati rice (page 107); Naan (page 99)

turn brown at the edges. Put in the mushrooms. Stir and fry until the mushrooms wilt. Now put in the tomatoes, ground coriander, ground cumin, turmeric, and cayenne. Stir and cook for 1 minute. Cover, turn the heat to low and let this mixture cook in its own juices for 10 minutes. Turn off the heat under the frying pan.

4. Bring the beans to a boil again. Cover,

turn the heat to low and simmer for 20-30 minutes. To this bean and water mixture, add the mushroom mixture, salt, black pepper and fresh coriander. Stir to mix and bring to a simmer. Simmer, uncovered, on a medium-low heat for another 30 minutes. Stir occasionally.

5. Remove the piece of cinnamon stick before serving.

Red kidney beans Punjabi-style

Punjabi rajma

RED KIDNEY BEANS, *Rajma*, are cooked slowly in Punjabi villages, often in the ashes of a *tandoor* or clay oven. I used to cook them for 4½ hours on top of the stove but have now found a much quicker method. This dish may also be made with aduki beans or an equal mixture of red kidney beans and aduki beans. These beans may be served with *Rogan josh* (Red lamb or beef stew, page 30) and an Indian bread.

PREPARATION TIME: 10 minutes, plus soaking and sitting
COOKING TIME: about 1¼ hours

Serves 4-6
175g (6oz) red kidney beans, washed, and drained
1.25 litres (2¼ pints) water
3 thin slices of unpeeled ginger, plus ½ teaspoon peeled and very finely chopped ginger
about 1 teaspoon salt
1½ tablespoons lemon juice
¼ teaspoon garam masala (page 13)
150 ml (5 fl oz) double cream
3 tablespoons ghee (page 16)
½ teaspoon cumin seeds
1 garlic clove, peeled and finely chopped
2 whole dried hot red chillies

1. Put the beans and 1.25 litres (2¼ pints) water into a heavy saucepan and bring to a boil. Turn the heat to low and simmer for 2 minutes. Turn off the heat and let the beans sit, uncovered, for 1 hour. Add the 3 slices of ginger to the beans and bring them to a boil again. Fast boil for 10 minutes, then cover, leaving the lid very slightly open. Turn the heat to low, and simmer gently for 1 hour. Discard the ginger slices.

2. You may now mash the beans against the sides of the pot or take half the beans and their liquid and purée them in a blender. Pour this purée back into the pan of beans. This gives the dish a pleasant texture. Add the salt, lemon juice, garam masala and cream. Stir to mix and check the seasonings.

3. Heat the ghee in a small frying pan over a medium flame. When it is hot, put in the cumin seeds. Two seconds later, put in the finely chopped garlic and the remaining chopped ginger. Stir and fry until the garlic browns lightly. Put in the red chillies. Stir them once and then pour the contents of the pan, ghee and seasonings, into the pot with the beans. Stir to mix.

4. The whole red chillies are not meant to be eaten.

Vale of Kashmir;
Inset: Making chapatis, Rajasthan, India

BREADS

THERE ARE ALL kinds of breads in India, most of them unleavened, eaten in the North at every single meal. Many of these everyday breads are made with a *very* finely ground wholewheat flour that we call *ata*. I find that the British flour that approximates *ata* best is wholemeal flour because it has just enough bran in it to give it body without making it too coarse for our soft, pliable breads. Of course, if you have access to Indian grocers and can buy *ata* (sometimes called *chapati* flour), do, by all means, use it.

Some of our breads, such as the poori, are deep-fried. The ideal utensil for this is the Indian *karhai* because it is very economical on oil and because it prevents hot oil from splashing on to the cooker. A deep frying pan may be used as a substitute.

Many other breads are cooked on a *tava*, a concave cast-iron plate that is heated before breads such as chapatis and parathas are slapped on to it. As I have suggested in the chapter on equipment, a cast-iron frying pan makes a perfectly adequate substitute.

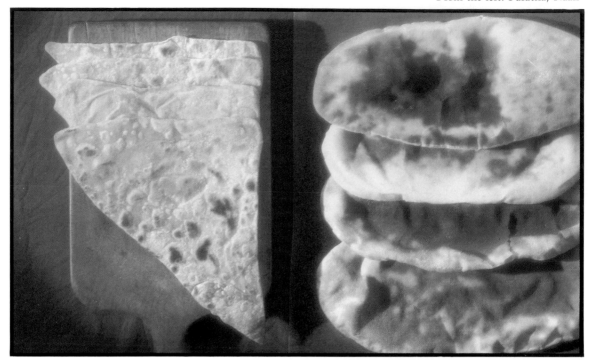

*L*ayered bread

Paratha

THESE ARE the triangular breads that we eat frequently with our meals and even pack up as school lunches for our children. With them, we have vegetables such as Spicy green beans (page 78) or The Lake Palace Hotel's aubergines cooked in the pickling style (page 77) and a meat dish.

PREPARATION TIME: 30 minutes, plus standing   COOKING TIME: 15-20 minutes

Makes about 12 and should serve 4-6
175 g (6 oz) plain wholemeal flour, sieved
185 g (6½ oz) plain flour, plus some for dusting
½ teaspoon salt
about 10 tablespoons vegetable oil or melted ghee (page 16)
150-200 ml (5-7 fl oz) water

1.   Put the two flours and the salt in a bowl. Dribble 2 tablespoons of the oil over the top. Rub the oil in with your fingertips until the mixture resembles coarse breadcrumbs. Slowly add anything from 150-200 ml (5-7 fl oz) water and gather the flour together to form a softish ball.

2.   Turn the ball on to a clean work surface.

Knead for about 10 minutes or until you have a smooth, soft but not sticky dough. Form a ball. Rub the ball with about ¼ teaspoon of the remaining oil and slip it into a polythene bag for 30 minutes or longer.

3.   Set a large cast-iron frying pan to heat on a medium-low flame. Meanwhile, knead the dough again and form 12 equal balls. Keep 11 of them covered while you work with the twelfth. Flatten this ball and dust it with some plain flour. Roll it out into a 15 cm (6 inch) round, dusting your work surface with flour whenever necessary. Spread ¼ teaspoon oil over the surface of the paratha and fold it in half. Spread about ⅛ teaspoon of oil over the surface of the half that is on top and fold it into half again to form a triangle. Roll out this triangle into a larger triangle with 18 cm (7 inch) sides. Dust with flour when necessary.

4.   Brush the hot frying pan with ¼ tea-

spoon of oil and slap the paratha on to it. Let the paratha cook for 1 minute. Now brush the top generously with 1 teaspoon of oil. The brushing will take about 30 seconds. Turn over the paratha and cook the other side for a minute or so. Both sides should have reddish-gold spots. Move the paratha around as you cook so all ends are exposed evenly to the heat.

5. Put the cooked paratha on a plate. Cover it either with an inverted plate or with a piece of aluminium foil. Make all the parathas in this way.

6. If parathas are not to be eaten right away, wrap them tightly in aluminium foil and refrigerate for a day or freeze. The whole, wrapped bundle of parathas may then be warmed through in a preheated oven (200°C, 400°F, Gas Mark 6) for 15-20 minutes.

Leavened oven bread

Naan

NAANS and other similar flat leavened breads are eaten all the way from the Caucasus down through north-western India. In India, the baking is done in very hot clay ovens or *tandoors*. The breads are slapped on to the inside walls and cook quite happily alongside skewered chickens. At home, where most of us do not have *tandoors*, naans can be baked by using both the oven and the grill. Naans may be cooked both with and without egg.
If you decide not to use the egg, just increase the yogurt by
about 4 tablespoons.
Naans may be eaten with almost any Indian meat or vegetable.

PREPARATION TIME: 30 minutes, plus standing   COOKING TIME: 20 minutes
OVEN: 240°C, 475°F, Gas Mark 9

Makes 6
150 ml (¼ pint) tepid milk
2 teaspoons caster sugar
2 teaspoons dried active yeast
450 g (1 lb) plain flour
½ teaspoon salt
1 teaspoon baking powder
2 tablespoons vegetable oil, plus a little extra
150 ml (5 fl oz) plain yogurt, lightly beaten
1 egg (size 1) lightly beaten

1. Put the milk into a bowl. Add 1 teaspoon of the sugar and the yeast. Stir to mix. Set aside for 15-20 minutes or until the yeast has dissolved and the mixture is frothy.

2. Sift the flour, salt and baking powder into a large bowl. Add the remaining sugar, yeast mixture, vegetable oil, yogurt and egg. Mix and form a ball of dough.

3. Empty the ball of dough on to a clean work surface and knead it for 10 minutes or more, until it is smooth and satiny. Form into a ball. Pour about ¼ teaspoon oil into a large bowl and roll the ball of dough in it. Cover the bowl with a piece of cling film and set aside in a warm, draught-free place for 1 hour or until the dough has doubled in bulk.

4. Preheat your oven to the highest temperature. Put the heaviest baking tray you own to heat in the oven. Preheat your grill.

5. Punch down the dough and knead it again. Divide it into 6 equal balls. Keep 5 of them covered while you work with the sixth. Roll this ball into a tear-shaped naan, about 25 cm (10 inches) by about 13 cm (5 inches).

6. Remove the hot baking tray from the oven and slap the naan on to it. Put it into the oven immediately for 3 minutes. It should puff up. Now place the baking tray and naan under the grill, about 7.5-10 cm (3-4 inches) away from the heat, for about 30 seconds or until the top of the naan browns slightly. Wrap the naan in a clean tea towel. Make all the naans in this way and serve hot.

*F*lat bread

Chapati

SOMETIMES small and delicate and at other times large and thick, this is the basic, flat and disc-like, Indian bread eaten over most of northern India. It is made out of a very finely ground wholewheat flour that is sold in Indian shops as *ata* or 'chapati flour'. I find that finely sifted wholemeal flour makes an adequate substitute. If you are using the wholemeal flour, make sure you sift it before you weigh it. Some people like to add a little bit of salt to the flour. This should be done before you make the dough.
Chapatis freeze well and thaw easily, without losing taste or texture.

PREPARATION TIME: 40 minutes, plus standing   COOKING TIME: about 20-25 minutes

Makes about 15

250 g (9 oz) sieved plain wholemeal flour, plus extra for dusting

175 ml (6 fl oz) water

1.   Put the flour into a bowl. Slowly add the water, gathering the flour together as you do so, to form a soft dough. Knead the dough for 6-8 minutes or until it is smooth. Put it into a bowl. Cover with a damp cloth and leave for 30 minutes.
2.   Set an Indian *tava* or any other cast-iron frying pan to heat over a medium-low flame for 10 minutes. When it is very hot, turn the heat to low.
3.   Knead the dough again and divide it, roughly, into 15 parts. It will be fairly sticky, so rub your hands with flour when handling it.
4.   Take 1 part of the dough and form a ball. Flour your work surface generously and roll the ball in it. Press down on the ball to make a patty. Now roll this patty out, dusting it very frequently with flour, until it is about 14 cm (5½ inches) in diameter.
5.   Pick up this chapati and pat it between your hands to shake off extra flour and then slap it on to the hot *tava* or frying pan. Let it cook on a low heat for about 1 minute. The underside should develop white spots. Turn the chapati over (I use my hands to do this but you could use a pair of tongs) and cook for about 30 seconds on the other side. Take the pan off the stove and put the chapati directly on top of the low flame. It should puff up in seconds.
6.   Turn over the chapati and let the other side sit on the flame for a few seconds. Put the chapati into a deep dish lined with a large napkin. Fold the napkin over the chapati. Make all the chapatis in this way.

From the left: Chapati; Poori

Deep-fried puffy bread

Poori

POORIS look like puffed-up balloons. They are crispy-soft, delicious, and may be eaten with almost all Indian meats, vegetables, and pulses. They are also easy to make. Rolled out discs of dough are put into hot oil – the oil *must* be hot or the pooris will not 'blister' and puff – and they cook magically in just a few seconds.

As pooris are best eaten hot, I have taught my entire family how to make them. I make three pooris per person. Then, if anyone wants more, they are told to go into the kitchen and make their own. And they do! Our poori dinners invariably turn into a 'happening' with flour-covered children and husband wandering in and out of the kitchen, rolling pin in hand and a look of great achievement on their faces.

A word of caution: as the cooking oil for pooris is hot, care should be taken not to splash it around. An Indian *karhai* is the safest and most economical utensil for deep-frying. If you do not have one, use a *deep* frying pan. Do not drop the poori into the oil from a great height or it will splash. Bring your hand as close as possible to the surface of the oil and lay the poori over it. Oil has no steam and will not burn you unless you touch it. When turning the poori over, bring it first to the edge of your utensil and then use the edge to help you turn it over. This, again, is to avoid splashes. Drain the cooked poori over the oil for a second or two before putting it in a platter. If you take these simple precautions (necessary for any deep-frying), poori-making can be fun.

PREPARATION TIME: 30 minutes, plus standing
COOKING TIME: about 15-20 minutes

Makes 12 pooris
100 g (4 oz) plain wholemeal flour, sieved
100 g (4 oz) plain flour
½ teaspoon salt
2 tablespoons vegetable oil, plus more for deep-frying
100 ml (3½ fl oz) water

1. Put the two flours and the salt into a bowl. Dribble the 2 tablespoons of oil over the top. Rub the oil in with your fingers so the mixture resembles coarse breadcrumbs. Slowly add the water to form a stiff ball of dough. Turn the ball on to a clean work surface. Knead it for 10-12 minutes or until it is smooth. Form a ball. Rub about ¼ teaspoon of oil on to the ball and slip it into a polythene bag. Set it aside for 30 minutes.

2. Knead the dough again, and divide it into 12 equal balls. Keep 11 of them covered while you work with the twelfth. Flatten this ball and roll it out into a 13-14 cm (5-5½ inch) round. If you have the space, roll out all the pooris and keep them in a single layer, covered with cling film.

3. Over a medium flame, set about 2.5 cm (1 inch) of oil to heat in a small, deep frying pan. Let it get very, very hot. Meanwhile, line a platter with paper towels.

4. Lift up one poori and lay it carefully over the surface of the hot oil. It may sink to the bottom but it should rise in seconds and begin to sizzle. Using the back of a slotted spoon, push the poori gently into the oil with tiny, *swift* strokes. Within seconds, the poori will puff up. Turn it over and cook the other side for about 10 seconds. Remove it with a slotted spoon and put it on the platter.

5. Make all the pooris in this way. The first layer on the platter may be covered with a layer of paper towel. More pooris can then be laid over the top. Serve the pooris hot.

Inset: Working in the rice fields, Kanchipuram,
Rice growing in the foothills of the Himalayas;
Southern India

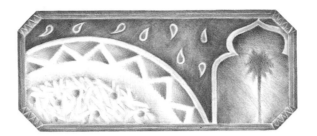

RICE

MY ENGLISH FRIENDS are always telling me that they cannot cook rice. They can hardly be blamed for their phobia. It starts, I think, with inadequate – inaccurate, in fact – instructions on rice packages that invariably suggest using far more water than rice really requires. The rice ends up by being mushy and the people who are cooking it often think that it is their fault. It is not.

There are, actually, many methods of cooking rice well. You will find several in the chapter that follows. Rice can be cooked like pasta, in a lot of boiling water until it is half done. Then it can be drained and 'dried off' in a slow oven. Rice can be cooked completely on top of the cooker with just the correct amount of water needed for absorption. Or you can start cooking rice on top of the cooker with just the amount of water needed for absorption and then finish it off in the oven. The method you choose depends upon the recipe and what you want the rice to do. I have used two types of rice in this chapter, long-grain (which could be labelled Patna or American long-grain) and basmati.

Basmati rice grows best in the foothills of the Himalaya Mountains, in both India and Pakistan. Actually, it too is a long-grain rice, only the grains are slender, delicate, naturally perfumed and somewhat more expensive! The best basmati rice is aged for a year before it is sold. This ageing increases its unusual, nutty aroma. While it is not necessary to pick over and wash packaged American rice (though washing will give it a better texture) basmati rice *must* be picked over, washed and soaked before cooking as it often contains small stones and other impurities.

The amazing thing about rice is that it can be cooked with almost any spice and combined with any vegetable, pulse or meat. It is, perhaps, the world's most amenable grain.

From the left: Plain easy-to-cook rice; South Indian-style light fluffy rice

If you are unsure about cooking rice, just follow my recipes carefully and you should not go wrong. There are a few things that are worth remembering when cooking rice:

1. Use a heavy pan with a very tight-fitting lid. If you have a tin-lined copper saucepan hanging decoratively in your kitchen, this is your chance to use it. An enamelled, cast-iron pan is also good for rice. I find that such saucepans generally have fairly loose-fitting lids. There is a very quick remedy for this. Just cover the saucepan tightly with a sheet of aluminium foil and then with its own lid. You can also make good rice in heavy, stainless steel saucepans. Any time you are unsure about the fitting of the lid, interpose a layer of aluminium foil between the saucepan and the lid. Be sure to crinkle the edges of the foil so that hardly any steam escapes. In many of my recipes, the rice ends up by cooking in steam. If too much of it escapes, the rice will not cook properly.

2. For best results, rice should be washed in several changes of water and then soaked for about 30 minutes before it is cooked. The washing gets rid of the starchy powder left over from the milling process. The soaking lets each grain absorb water so it sticks less to the next grain while it is cooking.

3. If you are cooking rice with just enough water or stock needed for absorption, what is the correct proportion of liquid to rice? I like to measure my rice in a clear measuring jug and I never use more than $1\frac{1}{2}$ parts liquid to 1 part rice. If I have soaked the rice, my ratio changes to $1\frac{1}{3}$ parts liquid to 1 part rice.

4. Sometimes I fry my rice before I add liquid to it. This also helps to keep the grains separate. When you fry rice, do it gently. Some types of rice grain, such as basmati, are very delicate, particularly after they have been soaked. If you fry too vigorously, the grains break up into small pieces.

5. Once I cover my rice saucepan with a lid, I like to cook it on a very, very low flame. If you cannot adjust the heat to very very low, then use a flameproof casserole, cover it tightly as instructed, and pop it into a preheated oven (160°C, 325°F, Gas Mark 3) for 25 minutes.

6. Resist any urge you may have to peep into a covered pan of rice before the cooking time is over. Precious steam will escape and the rice will cook unevenly.

7. If you have a thin layer of rice at the top of your pan that does not get cooked all the way through, while the rest of the rice does, then your lid is not tight enough. Use aluminium

foil between the pan and the lid next time around. Meanwhile, salvage your present situation by gently covering the partially cooked rice at the top with some fully cooked rice from the bottom. Add 1 or 2 tablespoons of water to the pan, cover tightly, this time using the foil, and cook for 10 minutes over very low heat.

8 When removing cooked rice from the pan, use a large slotted spoon. Either scrape out the rice gently, layer by layer, or else ease the spoon gently into the rice, lift out as much as you can, put it on a platter and then break up any lumps by pressing lightly with the back of the spoon.

Plain easy-to-cook rice

Saaday chaaval

THIS IS the quickest way of cooking American-style, packaged long-grain rice. It requires no washing and no soaking and may be served with any food.

PREPARATION TIME: 2 minutes   COOKING TIME: 20-25 minutes

Serves 6-8
long-grain rice measured to the 450 ml (¾ pint) level in a measuring jug
750 ml (1¼ pints) water
1 teaspoon salt (optional)
15 g (½ oz) unsalted butter (optional)

1. Combine the rice, water, salt and butter in a heavy-bottomed saucepan and bring to a boil. Cover very tightly, turn the heat to very, very low, and cook, undisturbed, for 15-20 minutes. Turn off the heat and let the saucepan rest, still covered and undisturbed, for another 5 minutes.

South Indian-style light fluffy rice

Dakshini chaaval

IN SOUTH INDIA, rice is generally parboiled in a large, round-bottomed, narrow-necked utensil with lots of water. When it is almost cooked, a cloth is tied to the mouth of the utensil and all the extra water drained out. (This water is later fed to the cows!) The pot is tilted so it lies on its belly over very low heat. A few live coals are placed on top of it as well to dry out the rice grains. Here is how the same rice may be made in a modern kitchen:

PREPARATION TIME: 5 minutes
COOKING TIME: 20 minutes   OVEN: 150°C, 300°F, Gas Mark 2

Serves 6-8
long-grain rice measured to the 450 ml (¾ pint) level in a measuring jug
2.75 litres (5 pints) water
1 teaspoon salt (optional)
15 g (½ oz) unsalted butter (optional)

1. Wash the rice in several changes of water and leave it to drain.

2. Fill a large saucepan with the water. Add the salt to it if you wish and bring it to a rolling boil. Empty the rice into the boiling water in a steady stream, stirring as you do so. Let the water come to a boil again. Boil rapidly for 10 minutes. Drain the rice in a colander.

3. Quickly put the rice into an ovenproof casserole. Lay the butter over it, cover tightly, and put the casserole into the oven for 10 minutes or until the rice is done. Mix the rice gently before you serve it.

Spiced basmati rice

Masaledar basmati

THIS IS one of the finest — and most delicate — basmati rice dishes. It may be served with an Indian meal or with English dishes such as roast lamb or grilled chicken.

PREPARATION TIME: 10 minutes, plus soaking and draining
COOKING TIME: about 25 minutes
OVEN: 160C, 325°F, Gas Mark 3

Serves 6-8
basmati rice measured to the 450 ml (¾ pint) level in a measuring jug
1.25 litres (2 pints) water
3 tablespoons vegetable oil
50 g (2 oz) onion, peeled and finely chopped
½ fresh, hot green chilli, finely chopped
½ teaspoon very finely chopped garlic
½ teaspoon garam masala (page 13)
1 teaspoon salt (a bit more if the stock is unsalted)
600 ml (1 pint) chicken stock

1.   Pick over the rice and put it into a bowl. Wash it in several changes of water. Drain. Pour the measured water over the rice and let it soak for 30 minutes. Leave to drain in a sieve for 20 minutes.

2.   Heat the oil in a heavy-bottomed saucepan over a medium flame. When it is hot, put in the onion. Stir and fry until the onion has browned lightly. Add the rice, green chilli, garlic, garam masala and salt. Stir gently for 3-4 minutes until all the grains are coated with oil. If the rice begins to stick to the bottom of the pan, turn down the heat slightly. Now pour in the stock and bring the rice to a boil. Cover with a very tight-fitting lid, turn the heat to very, very low and cook for 15 minutes.

3.   If you prefer, you could put the rice in a flameproof casserole and cook it in a preheated oven for 15 minutes.

From the top: Spiced basmati rice;
Plain basmati rice; Plain long-grain rice

Plain basmati rice

Basmati chaaval

I WAS brought up with this fine-grained rice. Now, as it has become quite expensive, it is only served at festive occasions and at parties.

PREPARATION TIME: 5 minutes, plus soaking
COOKING TIME: about 15 minutes

Serves 6-8
basmati rice measured to the 450 ml (¾ pint) level in a measuring jug
1.25 litres (2 pints) water, plus 600 ml (1 pint)
¾ teaspoon salt
15 g (½ oz) unsalted butter

1.   Pick over the rice and put it into a bowl. Wash in several changes of water. Drain. Pour about 1.25 litres (2 pints) of the water over the rice and let it soak for 30 minutes. Drain the rice thoroughly.

2.   Combine the rice, salt, butter and the 600 ml (1 pint) water in a heavy-bottomed pan. Bring to a boil. Cover with a tight-fitting lid, turn the heat to very low and cook for 10 minutes. Lift the lid, mix gently but quickly with a fork and cover again. Cook for 5 minutes or until the rice is tender.

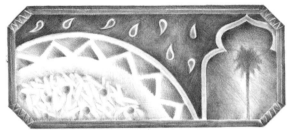

Plain long-grain rice

Barhiya chaaval

THIS RICE is slightly more elegant than the one in the preceding recipe mainly because it is washed and soaked before being cooked. These steps get rid of the starchy powder on the grains and help them to remain separate and unsplit.

PREPARATION TIME: 5 minutes, plus soaking and standing
COOKING TIME: 15-20 minutes

Serves 6-8
long-grain rice measured to the 450 ml (¾ pint) level in a measuring jug
1.25 ml (2 pints) water, plus 600 ml (1 pint)
1 teaspoon salt

1.   Put the rice into a bowl and wash in several changes of water. Drain. Leave to soak in about 1.25 litres (2 pints) of water for 30 minutes. Drain thoroughly.

2.   Put the drained rice, salt and 600 ml (1 pint) water into a heavy bottomed saucepan and bring to a boil. Cover with a very tight-fitting lid, turn the heat to very low and cook for 10-15 minutes. Take the saucepan off the flame and let it rest, still covered and undisturbed, for another 5 minutes.

Rice with yellow split peas

Khili hui khichri

KHICHRI is of ancient origin. It consists, basically, of rice and pulses cooked together and is served in most Indian homes in one of two forms, the 'wet', porridge-like version and the 'dry', grainy version. The recipe here is for the 'dry' khichri which my mother always referred to as khili hui khichri or 'the khichri which has bloomed'. This has the consistency of well-prepared rice. You could serve it with Kashmiri lamb stew (page 33) and an onion relish.

PREPARATION TIME: 10 minutes, plus soaking
COOKING TIME: 25-30 minutes

Serves 6

50 g (2 oz) yellow split peas, picked over, washed, and drained

450 ml (¾ pint) water, plus 1.2 litres (2 pints)

long-grain rice measured to the 450 ml (¾ pint) level in a measuring jug

3 tablespoon ghee (page 16) or vegetable oil

½ teaspoon cumin seeds

½ teaspoon garam masala (page 13)

1 teaspoon salt – or to taste

4 tablespoons finely chopped fresh coriander or parsley

600 ml (1 pint) chicken stock or water

1.   Soak the split peas in 450 ml (¾ pint) water for 3 hours. Drain. Wash the rice in several change of water and drain. Soak in 1.2 litres (2 pints) water for 1 hour. Drain.

2.   Heat the ghee in a heavy-bottomed saucepan over a medium flame. When it is hot, put in the cumin seeds. Stir them around for a few seconds. Now put in the drained split peas and the rice. Stir and fry gently for 2-3 minutes or until the grains are coated with the ghee. Add the garam masala, salt, and fresh coriander. Stir and fry for another minute or so. Add the chicken stock and bring to a boil. Cover tightly, turn the heat very, very low and cook for 10-15 minutes. Turn off the heat and let the saucepan sit, covered and undisturbed, for another 10 minutes.

3.   Stir gently with a slotted spoon or with a fork before serving.

Simple buttery rice with onion

Pyaz wali basmati chaaval

THIS SIMPLE METHOD of cooking rice makes it extremely versatile. You could serve it with Indian and English meals.

PREPARATION TIME: 5 minutes   COOKING TIME: 20-25 minutes

Serves 6

50 g (2 oz) unsalted butter

75 g (3 oz) onion, peeled and chopped

long-grain rice measured to the 450 ml (¾ pint) level in a measuring jug

1 teaspoon salt

750 ml (1¼ pints) water

1.   Melt the butter in a heavy-bottomed saucepan over a medium flame. When it is hot, put in the onion. Stir and fry it until it is almost translucent. Do not let it brown in the slightest. Put in the rice and the salt. Stir and fry gently for 1 minute. Pour in the water and bring to a boil. Cover tightly, turn the heat to very very low and let the rice cook for 15-20 minutes.

Rice with peas

Tahiri

THIS RICE DISH is flavoured, very mildly, with cumin seeds, making it suitable for almost any kind of meal.

PREPARATION TIME: 10 minutes, plus soaking
COOKING TIME: 25-30 minutes

Serves 6

long-grain rice measured to the 450 ml (¾ pint) level in a measuring jug

3 pints (1.75 litres) water

3 tablespoons vegetable oil

1 teaspoon cumin seeds

75 g (3 oz) onions, peeled and finely chopped

150-175 g (5-6 oz) fresh, shelled peas (or use frozen peas, thawed)

1 teaspoon salt

1. Wash the rice and drain it. Put the rice into a bowl. Add 1.2 litres (2 pints) of the water and soak it for 30 minutes. Drain.

2. Heat the oil in a heavy pan over a medium flame. When it is hot, put in the cumin seeds. Stir them about for 3 seconds. Now put in the chopped onions. Stir and fry them until they get flecked with brown spots. Add the peas, rice and salt. Stir gently for 3-4 minutes or until the peas and rice are coated with oil. Add the remaining water and bring to a boil. Cover very tightly, turn the heat to very very low and cook for 10-15 minutes. Turn off the flame and let the pan sit, covered and undisturbed, for another 5 minutes. Stir gently before serving.

Clockwise from top left: Rice with peas;
Rice with yellow split peas;
Simple buttery rice with onion

From the left: Mushroom pullao; Vegetable pullao

Mushroom pullao

Khumbi pullao

MY MOTHER used to make this dish with morel mushrooms. If you have some growing in your local woods, do, by all means, use them. Just slice them in half, lengthwise. You could also use the darker field mushrooms. In that case you would need to slice the caps. I tend to make this dish very frequently and find myself using the more easily available, cultivated mushrooms. It is still a superb dish and may be served with almost any meat dish in this book.

PREPARATION TIME: 15 minutes, plus soaking   COOKING TIME: 20-25 minutes

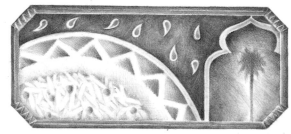

Serves 6	3 tablespoons vegetable oil
long-grain rice measured to the 450 ml (¾ pint) level in a measuring jug	1 garlic clove, peeled and finely chopped
1.75 litres (3 pints) water	½ teaspoon peeled and grated ginger
150 g (5 oz) mushrooms	¼ teaspoon garam masala (page 13)
50 g (2 oz) onion, peeled	1 teaspoon salt

1. Wash the rice in several changes of water and drain it. Put the rice into a bowl. Add 1.2 litres (2 pints) of water and soak for 30 minutes. Drain.

2. Wipe the mushrooms with a damp cloth or paper towel. Cut the mushrooms, from the caps down to the stems, into 3 mm (⅛ inch) thick slices. Cut the onion in half lengthwise, and then crosswise into very thin slices.

3. Heat the oil in a heavy saucepan over a medium flame. When it is hot, put in the onion and garlic. Stir and fry for about 2 minutes or until the onions begin to turn brown at the edges. Put in the mushrooms and stir for another 2 minutes. Now put in the rice, ginger, garam masala and salt. Turn the heat to medium-low. Stir and fry the rice for 2 minutes. Pour in 600 ml (1 pint) water and bring to a boil. Cover very tightly, turn the heat to very low and cook for 10-15 minutes. Turn off the heat and let the saucepan sit, covered and undisturbed, for 5 minutes.

Vegetable pullao

Sabzi pullao

SOMETIMES, when I want an an all-vegetarian meal, I serve this pullao with Black-eyed beans with mushrooms (page 94) and yogurt dish. It can, of course, be served with any meat.

PREPARATION TIME: 25 minutes, plus soaking and draining
COOKING TIME: 25-30 minutes

Serves 6
long-grain rice measured to the 450 ml (¾ pint) level in a measuring jug
1.2 litres (2 pints) water, plus 600 ml (1 pint)
100 g (4 oz) potato, peeled
40 g (1½ oz) carrot, peeled
40 g (1½ oz) fresh green beans
4 tablespoons vegetable oil
1 teaspoon cumin seeds
1¼ teaspoon salt
½ teaspoon ground turmeric
1 teaspoon ground cumin
1 teaspoon ground coriander
¼ teaspoon cayenne pepper
½ fresh hot green chilli, finely chopped
2 tablespoons very finely chopped fresh coriander
½ teaspoon peeled and very finely grated fresh ginger
1 garlic clove, peeled and mashed to a pulp

1. Put the rice into a bowl and wash it in several changes of water. Drain. Add the 1.2 litres (2 pints) water and leave it to soak for 30 minutes. Drain and leave in a sieve for 20 minutes.

2. Cut the potato and carrot into 5 mm (¼ inch) dice. Trim the green beans and cut them crosswise, at 5 mm (¼ inch) intervals.

3. Heat the oil in a heavy-bottomed saucepan over a medium heat. When it is hot, put in the cumin seeds. Let them sizzle for 5-6 seconds. Now put in the potato, carrot and green beans. Stir and fry gently for 1 minute. Turn the heat to medium-low and add the drained rice, salt, turmeric, ground cumin, ground coriander, cayenne, green chilli, fresh coriander, ginger and garlic. Stir and fry the rice for 2-3 minutes. Add the water and bring to a boil.

4. Cover very tightly, turn the heat to very, very low, and cook for 10-15 minutes. Turn off the heat and let the saucepan sit, covered and undisturbed, for another 10 minutes.

Sweet yellow rice

Meetha pullao

THIS WONDERFUL sweet shining rice may be eaten by itself as a dessert, with hot, spicy Indian dishes or even with English food such as baked ham and roast goose.

PREPARATION TIME: 5 minutes, plus soaking and draining
COOKING TIME: 25 minutes   OVEN: 150°C, 300°F, Gas Mark 2

Serves 4	2.5 cm (1 inch) piece of cinnamon stick
½ teaspoon saffron threads	¼ teaspoon liquid yellow food colouring
2 tablespoons warm milk	½ teaspoon salt
basmati rice measured to the 250 ml (8 fl oz) level in a measuring jug	15 g (½ oz) blanched, slivered almonds
1.5 litres (2½ pints) water	1 tablespoon sultanas
50 g (2 oz) ghee (page 16)	90 g (3½ oz) sugar, or to taste
4 cardamom pods	silver vark (page 15) (optional)

1.   Put the saffron into a small heavy frying pan set over a medium flame. Stir it about until the threads turn a few shades darker. Put the milk into a small cup and crumble the saffron into it. Set it aside for 3 hours.
2.   Wash the rice in several changes of water and drain it. Leave it to soak in 1.25 litres (2 pints) of water for 30 minutes, then leave it to drain for 20 minutes.
3.   Heat the ghee in a wide, heavy flameproof casserole over a medium flame. When it is hot, put in the cardamom and cinnamon. Stir them about for 1 second. Now pour in the rice. Stir and fry the rice gently for about 3 minutes, turning the heat down slightly if it begins to catch. Add the remaining 300 ml (½ pint) water, yellow colouring and salt. Turn the heat back to medium. Gently stir and cook the rice until all the water is absorbed. Put in the saffron milk, almonds, sultanas and sugar. Stir to mix, cover very tightly, and put the casserole in the oven for 10 minutes. Remove from the oven and stir to mix.
4.   Remove the cardamom and cinnamon before serving. If liked, silver vark can be placed on the rice with a few extra sultanas and nuts.

Aromatic yellow rice

Peelay chaaval

YOU MAY use either basmati rice or American long-grain rice for this recipe. The yellow colour comes from ground turmeric. I like to serve it with Chicken in a red sweet pepper sauce (page 52).

PREPARATION TIME: 5 minutes, plus soaking   COOKING TIME: 25-30 minutes

Serves 6	¾ teaspoon ground turmeric
long-grain or basmati rice measured to the 450 ml (¾ pint) level in a measuring jug	3-4 cloves
1.2 litres (2 pints) water	2.5 cm (1 inch) piece of cinnamon stick
1¼ teaspoons salt	3 bay leaves
	3 tablespoons unsalted butter

Clockwise from top left:
Sweet yellow rice; Aromatic yellow rice;
Lamb and rice casserole (page 114)

1. Put the rice in a bowl and wash it in several changes of water. Drain. Pour 1.2 litres (2 pints) of fresh water over the rice and let it soak for 30 minutes. Drain the rice in a sieve.

2. Combine the drained rice, 600 ml (1 pint) water, salt, turmeric, cloves, cinnamon and bay leaves in a heavy-bottomed saucepan and bring to a boil. Cover with a tight-fitting lid, turn the heat to very, very low and cook for 10-15 minutes. Let the saucepan rest, covered and undisturbed, for 10 minutes.

3. Cut the butter into small dice, add to the rice and mix them in gently with a fork. Remove the whole spices before serving.

Lamb and rice casserole

Mughlai biryani

Pictured on
page 113

BIRYANIS are grand, festive casseroles in which partially cooked rice is layered over cooked meat. Orange saffron milk is dribbled over the top, thereby colouring some grains yellow while leaving others white, and the dish set to bake in a slow oven. As it cooks, the biryani gets quite perfumed with saffron.

These days, with saffron being as expensive as it is, many people, even in India, use yellow food colouring as a substitute. You may do so too if you wish. Just use 1 teaspoon yellow liquid food colouring diluted with 1 teaspoon water instead of the saffron and warm milk.

Soaking the rice in salted water for long periods, from 3 to 24 hours, is an ancient trick that the Persians used to get rice grains as white – and as separate from each other – as possible. These shining white grains then contrast even better with those tinted with saffron.

A biryani is really a meal in itself and may be eaten with just a yogurt dish, such as Yogurt with aubergines (page 119), and a relish, such as my Tomato, onion, and green coriander relish (page 124). However, since biryanis are generally served at feasts and banquets, we tend to be lavish. At such occasions, it would not be at all amiss to serve the condiments suggested above *as well as* Chicken in a red sweet pepper sauce (page 52) and Cauliflower with onion and tomato (page 82).

PREPARATION TIME: 50 minutes, plus soaking
COOKING TIME: 2¼ hours
OVEN: 150°C, 300°F, Gas Mark 2

Serves 6	*750 g (1½ lb) boned shoulder of lamb, cut into 2.5 cm (1 inch) cubes*
long-grain or basmati rice measured to the 450 ml (¾ pint) level in a measuring jug	*250 ml (8 fl oz) plain yogurt*
5.75 litres (9¾ pints) water, plus 3 tablespoons	*5-6 cloves*
about 3 tablespoons salt	*½ teaspoon black peppercorns*
1 teaspoon saffron threads	*½ teaspoon cardamom seeds*
2 tablespoons warm milk	*1 teaspoon cumin seeds*
3 medium onions, peeled	*1 teaspoon coriander seeds*
4 garlic cloves, peeled	*2.5 cm (1 inch) piece of cinnamon stick*
1 × 2 cm (¾ inch) cube of fresh ginger, peeled and coarsely chopped	*about ⅙ of a nutmeg*
4 tablespoons blanched, slivered almonds	*¼ teaspoon cayenne pepper*
200 ml (7 fl oz) vegetable oil	*25 g (1 oz) unsalted butter, cut into 8 pieces*
3 tablespoons sultanas	*3 hard boiled eggs, shelled and at room temperature*

1.   Wash the rice in several changes of water. Drain it and put it into a large bowl. Add 2 litres (3½ pints) water and 1 tablespoon salt. Mix and soak for 3 hours.

2.   Put the saffron threads into a small heavy, preferably cast-iron, frying pan set over a medium flame. Toss the threads about until they turn a few shades darker. Put the warm milk into a small cup. Crumble the saffron into the warm milk and let it soak for 3 hours.

3.   Cut 2 of the onions in half lengthwise, and then cut the halves into fine half-rings. Set these aside. Chop the remaining onion very coarsely. Put this chopped onion, garlic,

ginger, 2 tablespoons of the almonds and 3 tablespoons water into the container of an electric blender. Blend until you have a paste.

4.   Heat 6 tablespoons of the oil in a 25 cm (10 inch), preferably non-stick, frying pan over a medium-high flame. When it is hot, put in the onion half-rings. Stir and fry them until they are brown and crisp. Remove them with a slotted spoon and spread them out on a plate lined with paper towels.

5.   Put the sultanas into the same oil. Remove them as soon as they turn plump – which happens immediately. Put the sultanas on another plate lined with absorbent paper. Put the remaining almonds into the oil. Stir and fry them until they are golden. Remove them with a slotted spoon and spread them out beside the sultanas. Set aside for the garnish.

6.   Now put the meat cubes, a few at a time, into the same hot oil and brown them. As each batch gets done, put it into a bowl.

7.   Add the remaining oil to the frying pan and turn the heat to medium. When it is hot, put in the onion-garlic-ginger-almond paste from the blender. Fry, stirring all the time, until the paste turns a medium brown colour. If it sticks slightly to the bottom of the pan, sprinkle in a little water and keep stirring. Re-

Krishna enthroned
Pahari School, circa 1710

turn the meat and any accumulated juices to the pan. Add the yogurt, 1 tablespoon at a time, stirring well between each addition. Now put in 1¼ teaspoons salt and 150 ml (¼ pint) water. Mix and bring to a simmer. Cover, turn the heat to low and simmer for 30 minutes.

8.   While the meat is cooking, put the cloves, peppercorns, cardamom seeds, cumin seeds, coriander seeds, cinnamon and nutmeg into the container of a spice grinder or a clean coffee grinder. Grind finely.

9.   When the meat has cooked for 30 minutes, add all the spice from the spice grinder as well as the cayenne and mix well. Cover again and continue to cook on a low heat for another 30 minutes. Remove the lid, raise the heat to medium, and cook, stirring all the time, until you have about 200 ml (7 fl oz) of thick sauce left at the bottom of the pan. Turn off the heat and spoon off as much grease as possible. The meat should be pretty well cooked by now.

10.   Spread out the meat and the sauce in the bottom of a heavy casserole. Cover and keep warm.

11.   Bring 3.5 litres (6 pints) of the water to a rolling boil in a large saucepan. Add 1½ tablespoons salt. Drain the rice and rinse it under running water. Slowly scatter the rice into the boiling water. Bring to a boil again and boil rapidly for exactly 6 minutes. Then drain the rice.

12.   Work fast now. Put the rice on top of the meat, piling it up in the shape of a hill. Take a chopstick or the handle of a long spoon and make a hole, 2.5 cm (1 inch) wide, going down like a well from the peak of the rice hill to the bottom. Dribble the saffron milk in streaks along the sides of the hill. Lay the pieces of butter on the sides of the hill, and scatter 2 tablespoons of the browned onions over it as well. Cover first with aluminium foil, sealing the edges well, and then with a lid. Bake in a preheated oven for 1 hour.

13.   Remove the dish from the oven. If left in a warm place, the rice will stay hot for 30 minutes.

14.   Just before you serve, quarter the eggs, lengthwise. Mix the contents of the rice pan gently. Serve the rice on a warmed platter, garnished with the eggs, the remaining browned onions, the sultanas and almonds.

Pushkar lake and village, Rajasthan

RELISHES CHUTNEYS AND PICKLES

WE LIKE to perk up our meals in India with a variety of condiments. Their function, apart from teasing the palate with their sharp contrasts of sweet, sour, hot and salty flavours, is to balance out the meal with added protein and vitamins.

Sometimes these condiments can be quite simple — cucumber wedges seasoned quickly with salt, pepper, cayenne and lemon juice or chopped onions and tomatoes. At other times we can serve pickles that have taken weeks or months to mature. Some condiments, such as the *Hare dhaniye ki chutney* (Fresh coriander chutney) or the *Gajar ka salad* (Gujerati carrot salad), should be eaten within 48 hours. Others, such as the *Sev, aroo, aur kubani ki chutney* (Apple, peach and apricot chutney) and the *Phool gobi aur mooli ka achaar* (Cauliflower and white radish pickle) may be kept for a year.

Yogurt relishes fall into another category. They can be condiments or they can be substantial dishes by themselves. Almost any herb or vegetable, from mint to potatoes, can be put into yogurt. Whenever I am serving an all-Indian meal, I nearly always serve a yogurt relish because it provides a cooling contrast.

Plain yogurt

Dahi

YOGURT is used in India for marinating meats as it tenderizes them; as a tart, creamy flavouring and as an ingredient for sauces. Since it is rich in protein it is also eaten at almost every meal, either plain or mixed with seasonings and vegetables. It is a food that is easy to digest, far easier than milk. It is also considered a food that 'settles' the stomach, especially when combined with plain rice. Naturally, few respectable Indian homes are ever without it. Most of the time it is made at home, although it can be bought from the bazaar as well.

To make yogurt at home, you need milk, preferably skimmed, and some 'starter'. This 'starter' is a few tablespoons of borrowed, leftover or bought yogurt. You also need a warm temperature that hovers between 30°-38°C (85°-100°F). This is the temperature at which yogurt sets best. As this is not England's temperature normally, it has to be approximated.

PREPARATION TIME: 5 minutes, plus cooling and setting

Makes 1 litre (1¾ pints)
1 litre (1¾ pints) skimmed milk
2 tablespoons plain yogurt

1. Bring the milk to a boil in a heavy saucepan. As soon as the milk begins to rise, remove the saucepan from the heat. Let the milk cool to somewhere between 38°-43°C (100°-110°F). It should feel warm to the touch. If a film forms over the top, just stir it in.
2. Put the yogurt into a 1.25 litre (2 pint) stainless steel or non-metallic bowl and beat it with a whisk until it is smooth and creamy. Slowly add the warm milk, a little at a time, stirring as you do so. Cover the bowl and then wrap it in an old blanket or shawl without tilting it. Set it aside in a warm place free of draughts for 6-8 hours or until it has set.
3. Store the yogurt in a refrigerator. It should stay fresh for 4-5 days.

From the top: Yogurt with aubergines; Plain yogurt; Yogurt with cucumber and mint

Yogurt with aubergines

Baigan ka raita

HERE IS a soothing, cooling, and exceedingly simple way to serve aubergines. I like to serve this with Delhi-style lamb cooked with potatoes (page 36), Gujerati-style green beans (page 78) and either rice or an Indian bread.

PREPARATION TIME: 10 minutes   COOKING TIME: 15 minutes

Serves 6

500 g (1¼ lb) aubergines, peeled and cut into 2.5 cm (1 inch) cubes

450 ml (¾ pint) plain yogurt

¾ teaspoon salt, or to taste

freshly ground black pepper

⅛ teaspoon cayenne pepper (optional)

1 spring onion, washed and cut into paper-thin rounds

1 tablespoon finely chopped fresh mint

a few mint leaves, to garnish

1.   Bring water in the base of a steamer to the boil. (If you do not have a steamer, set a steaming trivet or a colander inside a large saucepan. Pour water into the saucepan in such a way that it stays just below the lowest part of the trivet or colander.)

2.   Put the aubergine cubes into the top of the steamer (or into the trivet or colander), cover and steam over high heat for 10 minutes. Top up with more boiling water if necessary.

3.   While the aubergine pieces are steaming, put the yogurt into a bowl and beat it lightly with a fork or a whisk until it is smooth and creamy. Add the salt, pepper, cayenne, spring onion and mint. Mix with a fork.

4.   Lift out the steamed aubergine pieces and mash them with a fork. Spread out the aubergine on a plate and leave to cool somewhat (or else the yogurt will curdle).

5.   Fold the aubergine into the yogurt and garnish with mint leaves.

Yogurt with cucumber and mint

Kheere ka raita

HERE IS a cooling yogurt dish that can be served with all Indian meals.

PREPARATION TIME: 5 minutes

Serves 6

600 ml (1 pint) plain yogurt

13 cm (5 inch) piece cucumber, peeled and coarsely grated

2 tablespoons finely chopped fresh mint

½ teaspoon ground, roasted cumin seeds (page 13)

¼ teaspoons cayenne pepper

1 teaspoon salt

freshly ground black pepper

1.   Put the yogurt into a bowl. Beat lightly with a fork or whisk until it is smooth and creamy. Add all the other ingredients and mix. Cover and refrigerate until ready to eat.

Gujerati-style yogurt with potatoes

Batata nu raita

THIS IS an Indian potato salad except that we use seasoned yogurt as a dressing instead of mayonnaise or a vinaigrette. In order to make the yogurt very thick and creamy, it is generally hung up in a cheesecloth for 1 hour. You may omit this step if you are in a rush. You will, of course, end up with a more 'flowing' sauce, rather than one which clings to the potatoes. It may be served with Minced meat with peas (page 24) and an Indian bread.

PREPARATION TIME: 10 minutes, plus cooling and draining
COOKING TIME: 30 minutes

Serves 6

275 g (10 oz) potatoes

450 ml (¾ pint) plain yogurt

½ teaspoon salt

freshly ground black pepper

2 tablespoons vegetable oil

1 teaspoon cumin seeds

⅛ teaspoon cayenne pepper, or to taste

1 tablespoon finely chopped fresh coriander or parsley, to garnish (optional)

1. Boil the potatoes in their jackets. Drain them and let them cool for at least 1 hour.
2. Set a sieve over a bowl and line it with a 38-40 cm (15-16 inch) square of doubled cheesecloth or a clean tea towel. Put the yogurt into the cheesecloth. Now bring the four corners of the cheesecloth together. Use one of the corners to tie the cheesecloth into a bundle. Hang this bundle somewhere so it can drip for 1 hour. I usually hang it from the tap in my sink. Do not squeeze the cheesecloth. Just let it drip on its own.
3. Empty the yogurt into a bowl. Add about ¼ teaspoon salt and some black pepper. Beat lightly with a fork or a whisk until the yogurt is smooth and creamy. Taste for seasoning and adjust it if necessary.
4. Peel the potatoes and cut them into 2 cm (¾ inch) dice. Heat the oil in a frying pan (non-stick is best) over a medium flame. When it is hot, put in the cumin seeds. Let the cumin seeds sizzle for 3-4 seconds. Now put in the diced potatoes, about ⅓ teaspoon salt, some black pepper and the cayenne. Stir and cook the potatoes for about 4 minutes. Taste a

potato piece for seasoning. You may make this dish as hot as you like. Take the frying pan off the heat; let the potatoes cool for 5 minutes.
5. Pour the contents of the frying pan — oil, spices and potatoes — into the bowl with the yogurt. Stir to mix and garnish, if you like, with fresh coriander or parsley.

16th century illustration to the Romance of Amir Hamza, during Akhbar's period, Northern India

From the left: Gujerati-style yogurt with potatoes; Fresh coriander chutney

Fresh coriander chutney

Hare dhaniye ki chutney

THIS IS the kind of chutney that is made fresh in our homes every day. Apart from its sharp, perky taste, it is exceedingly rich in Vitamins A and C as well as in chlorophyll. We eat small amounts – 1-2 teaspoons – with our meals just as you might eat mustard with sausages. It also serves as an excellent dip for snacks such as samosas.

When making the chutney, use just the top, leafy sections of the coriander plant. The stems get too stringy when pulverized.

PREPARATION TIME: 5 minutes

Serves 4-6
75 g (3 oz) fresh coriander leaves, coarsely chopped
½-1 fresh hot green chilli, coarsely chopped
1½ tablespoons lemon juice
½ teaspoons salt
½ teaspoon ground roasted cumin seeds (page 13)
freshly ground black pepper

1.   Combine all the ingredients in the container of an electric blender. Blend, pushing down with a rubber spatula several times, until you have a paste. Empty the paste into a small glass or other non-metallic bowl.

Apple, peach and apricot chutney

Sev, aroo, aur kubani ki chutney

THIS SUPERB fruity sweet-and-sour chutney has the thick consistency of a preserve and may be bottled and kept for long periods. Those who like their chutney very hot can add up to 1½ teaspoons of cayenne pepper. It may be served with all Indian meals as well as with gammon roasts, pork chops, and ham.

PREPARATION TIME: 15 minutes, plus cooling
COOKING TIME: 30 minutes

Makes about 750 ml (1¼ pints)	2 × 2.5 cm (1 inch) cubes of fresh ginger, peeled and finely grated
500 g (1¼ lb) cooking apples, peeled, cored and coarsely chopped	400 ml (14 fl oz) white wine vinegar
100 g (4 oz) dried peaches, quartered	400 g (14 oz) caster sugar
100 g (4 oz) dried apricots	2 teaspoons salt
50 g (2 oz) sultanas	½ teaspoon cayenne pepper
6 garlic cloves, peeled and mashed to a pulp	

1. Combine all the ingredients in a heavy stainless steel or porcelain-lined pan and bring them to a boil. Turn the heat to medium-low and cook, keeping up a fairly vigorous simmer, for about 30 minutes or until you have a thick, jam-like consistency. Stir frequently and turn down the heat slightly when the chutney thickens as it could stick to the bottom of the pan.

2. Let the chutney cool. It will thicken more as it cools. Pour into a clean jar and cover with a non-metallic lid. Store in a cool place or keep in the refrigerator.

From the left: Apple, peach and apricot chutney; Gujerati carrot salad; Carrot and onion salad

Gujerati carrot salad

Gajar ka salad

THIS SIMPLE, lightly spiced, easy-to-make salad may be served with Indian meals – or with something as British as grilled sausages! There are many variations to it which you might like to try out on your family and friends. You could, for example, leave out the lemon juice. This highlights the natural sweetness of the carrots. Or you could add 2 tablespoons of sultanas which you should soak in hot water for 2-3 hours first.

PREPARATION TIME: 5 minutes
COOKING TIME: 2 minutes

Serves 4
350 g (12 oz) carrots, trimmed, peeled and grated coarsely
¼ teaspoon salt
2 tablespoons vegetable oil
1 tablespoon black mustard seeds
2 teaspoons lemon juice

1. In a bowl, toss the grated carrots with the salt. Heat the oil in a very small pan over a medium flame. When it is very hot, put in the mustard seeds. As soon as the mustard seeds begin to pop (this takes just a few seconds) pour the contents of the pan – oil and seeds – over the carrots. Add the lemon juice and toss.
2. Serve this salad at room temperature or chill it in the refrigerator and serve cold.

Carrot and onion salad

Gajar aur pyaz ka salad

THIS SALAD is made with the deep red, beetroot-like 'bleeding' carrot that is found in north India during the winter months. I have substituted the ordinary orange carrot. It may be served with nearly all Indian meals.

PREPARATION TIME: 15 minutes
COOKING TIME: 5-10 minutes

Serves 6
3 carrots, total weight about 225 g (8 oz)
75 g (3 oz) onion, peeled
2.25 litres (4 pints) water
¾ teaspoon salt
freshly ground black pepper
4 teaspoons lemon juice
⅛-¼ teaspoon cayenne pepper
½ teaspoon peeled and finely grated fresh ginger

1. Peel the carrots and cut them, crosswise and at a diagonal, into 3 mm (⅛ inch) thick oval slices. Cut the slices, lengthwise, into 3 mm (⅛ inch) wide strips.
2. Halve the onion lengthwise, and then cut it crosswise into 3 mm (⅛ inch) thick slices.
3. Bring the water to a rolling boil. Throw in the carrots. Bring to a boil again. Boil rapidly for 2 seconds only. Drain the carrots immediately and rinse them under cold running water. Drain again.
4. Combine the carrots, onion, salt, black pepper, lemon juice, cayenne and ginger. Stir.
5. This salad may be served as soon as it is made or several hours later. It may be served at room temperature or cold.

123

Cauliflower and white radish pickle

Phool gobi aur mooli ka achaar

THIS IS one of the simplest Indian pickles. It does take several days to mature, so you have to be patient. Small amounts of it may be served at all Indian meals.
You may substitute turnip slices for the white radish in this recipe. The mustard seeds and oil, however, are essential. I heat the mustard oil before I use it in the pickle, because this process transforms it from a pungent oil to a sweet one.

PREPARATION TIME: 15 minutes, plus maturing
COOKING TIME: 2 minutes

Makes enough to fill a 900 ml (1½ pint) jar
225 g (8 oz) cauliflower
225 g (8 oz) white radish (mooli)
4 teaspoons black mustard seeds
120 ml (4 fl oz) mustard oil
2 teaspoons salt
½ teaspoon ground turmeric
½-1 teaspoon cayenne pepper

1.   Cut the cauliflower into florets about 2.5-4 cm (1-1½ inches) across at the head and 4-5 cm (1½-2 inches) long. Peel the radish and cut it into 7.5 mm (⅓ inch) thick rounds. If the diameter of the slices is more than 2.5 cm (1 inch), halve or quarter them.

2.   Grind the mustard seeds coarsely in a coffee grinder or other spice grinder.
3.   Heat the oil in a small saucepan or frying pan over a medium heat. Immediately it gets very, very hot, turn off the heat and let it cool. (Remember to take very great care with hot oil – stand over the oil as it cools.)
4.   Put the cut vegetables into a bowl. Add the ground mustard seeds, salt, turmeric and cayenne. Mix well. Add the oil and mix again. Empty the contents of the bowl into a 1.25 litre (2 pint) glass or ceramic jar and cover it with a non-metallic lid. For the next few days, keep the jar in a warm sunny spot in the day time. This pickle will take 4-5 days to mature in the summer and about 8 days in the winter.
5.   Make sure you shake the jar at least 3-4 times a day. When the pickle is sour enough for your liking, it is ready. Store it in a cool place.

Tomato, onion and green coriander relish

Cachumber

THIS TASTY relish complements almost all Indian meals.

PREPARATION TIME: 10 minutes

Serves 4-6	¾ teaspoon salt
225 g (8 oz) tomatoes	2 tablespoons lemon juice
75 g (3 oz) onion, peeled	½ teaspoon cayenne pepper
4 heaped tablespoons chopped fresh coriander or parsley	½ teaspoon ground roasted cumin seeds (page 13)

1.   Cut the tomatoes and onions into 5 mm (¼ inch) dice and put them into a non-metallic serving bowl. Add all the other ingredients and mix.

Onion relish

Pyaz ka laccha

THIS IS one of those relishes that may be served with almost every Indian meal. It may be familiar to you from Indian restaurants where it is sometimes described as 'onion chutney'.

PREPARATION TIME: 5 minutes, plus standing

Serves 4

100 g (4 oz) onion, peeled

¾ teaspoon salt

4 teaspoons lemon juice

¼ teaspoon paprika (the redder the better)

⅛ teaspoon cayenne pepper

1.   Cut the onion crosswise into paper-thin rings. Put the rings into a bowl. Add all the other ingredients. Toss and mix. Set aside for 30 minutes (or more) before eating in order to let the flavours blend.

Illustration: A sweetmeat maker's shop, Patna, 19th century
From the left: Cauliflower and white radish pickle;
Tomato, onion and green coriander relish;
Onion relish

Cowasji Jehangir Hall, Bombay, at night

126

SOUPS SNACKS SAVOURIES AND SWEETS

INDIANS love to munch. Whether they are on buses or trains, in cinemas or parks, they can be spotted opening up newspaper cones, unwrapping tea-cloth bundles or easing eager hands into terracotta pots. Good things are hidden inside that can be nibbled for the satisfaction of the soul.

Take samosas, for instance, those triangular savoury pastries. The best place to eat them is on the street, when the odours wafting from the samosa-makers become too overwhelming to resist. All kinds of kebabs, marinated and grilled meat cubes, are also sold at open stalls.

All workers in India stop for tea, a custom not too different from the British one. But what is served, *is* a bit different. There would be tea of course, perhaps *Masala chai* (Spiced tea) or coffee. Then, an odd assortment might appear — samosas, fried cashews and, to sweeten the mouth, some *Gajar ka halva* (Carrot halva)!

All these dishes have been included in this chapter. There are also snacks that may be served with drinks, such as *Chhote kofte* (Delicious cocktail koftas), meatballs that lend themselves very well to having toothpicks stuck in them and *Aloo ka tala hua laccha* (Spicy matchstick potato crisps).

I have included some soups in this chapter as well. Even though we do not, as a nation drink soups, most westernized Indians have happily adapted soups from other countries to suit their own tastes.

Everyday meals in India generally end with fresh fruit — a perfect conclusion to a spicy meal. Desserts and sweetmeats are usually reserved for festive occasions. A wedding banquet invariably brings large vats filled with *kulfi* — Indian ice cream — and at religious festivals some variety of halva is nearly always served.

127

Green soup

Hara shorva

THIS IS India's version of cream of pea soup. It is delicate and quite delicious.

PREPARATION TIME: 10 minutes
COOKING TIME: 40 minutes

Makes 1.5 litres (2½ pints) and serves 5-6
100 g (4 oz) potato, peeled and roughly diced
75 g (3 oz) onion, peeled and coarsely chopped
1.2 litres (2 pints) chicken stock
1 × 2 cm (¾ inch) cube of fresh ginger, peeled
½ teaspoon ground coriander
2 teaspoons ground cumin
5 tablespoons chopped fresh coriander
½ fresh hot green chilli
275 g (10 oz) shelled peas
¾ teaspoon salt (more if the stock is unsalted)
1 tablespoon lemon juice
½ teaspoon ground roasted cumin seeds (page 13)
150 ml (¼ pint) double cream

1.   Combine the potato, onion, chicken stock, ginger, ground coriander and ground cumin in a saucepan and bring to a boil. Cover, turn the heat to low and simmer for 30 minutes. Remove the cube of ginger and discard. Add the fresh coriander, chilli, peas, salt, lemon juice, and roasted cumin. Bring to a boil and simmer, uncovered, for 2-3 minutes or until the peas are just tender.
2.   Empty the soup into the container of an electric blender in two or three batches and blend until it is smooth.
3.   Put the soup into a clean saucepan. Add the cream and bring to a simmer to heat the soup through. Serve immediately.

From the top: Chicken mulligatawny soup;
Green soup; Plain long-grain rice (page 106)

Chicken mulligatawny soup

Masalay dar murgh ka shorva

THERE ARE many soupy dishes in India that are served with rice. It was probably one of these that inspired Anglo-Indian communities three centuries ago to create a soup that had Indian spices and ingredients in it, yet could be served at the start of a meal.

There are hundreds of recipes for mulligatawny soup in India, all slightly different. For this book, I have chosen one in which the base is a purée of red split lentils (*masoor dal*). It is a hearty soup that can almost be a meal in itself. I often have it for lunch with a simple green salad. It is traditional to have some plain boiled rice with this soup. I usually serve it on the side, in small quantities.

PREPARATION TIME: 20 minutes
COOKING TIME: about 1¼ hours

Serves 4-6

175 g (6 oz) red split lentils, washed and drained

1.2 litres (2 pints) chicken stock

½ teaspoon ground turmeric

100 g (4 oz) potato

5 garlic cloves, peeled

1 × 3 cm (1¼ inch) cube of fresh ginger, peeled and coarsely chopped

4½ tablespoons water, plus 250 ml (8 fl oz)

1 chicken breast, boned and skinned, net weight about 200 g (7 oz)

1¼ teaspoons salt

freshly ground black pepper

3 tablespoons vegetable oil

1 teaspoon ground cumin

1 teaspoon ground coriander

⅛-¼ teaspoon cayenne pepper

about 1 tablespoon lemon juice (you might want more)

1.   Combine the lentils, chicken stock and turmeric in a heavy, medium saucepan and bring to a boil. Cover, leaving the lid just very slightly open, turn the heat to low and simmer gently for 30 minutes.

2.   While the soup simmers, peel the potato and cut it into 1 cm (½ inch) dice. When the soup has cooked for 30 minutes add the potato. Cover, leaving the lid slightly open, and continue simmering for another 30 minutes.

3.   During this second simmering period, put the garlic and ginger into the container of an electric blender. Add 4½ tablespoons water and blend until you have a smooth paste.

4.   Remove all the fat from the chicken breast and cut it into 1 cm (½ inch) dice. Put the chicken into a bowl. Sprinkle ¼ teaspoon salt and some black pepper over it. Toss to mix.

5.   Once the soup base has finished cooking, it needs to be puréed. I do this in a blender, in 3 batches. Put the puréed soup into a bowl. Add 1 teaspoon salt to it and mix.

6.   Rinse and wipe out your soup saucepan. Pour in the oil and set it over a medium flame. When the oil is hot, put in the garlic-ginger paste, cumin, coriander and cayenne. Fry, stirring constantly, until the spice mixture is slightly browned and separates from the oil.

7.   Put in the chicken pieces. Stir and fry for another 2-3 minutes or until the chicken pieces turn quite opaque. Add 250 ml (8 fl oz) water and bring to a boil. Cover, turn the heat to low, and simmer for 3 minutes or until the chicken is cooked. Pour in the puréed soup and the lemon juice. Stir to mix and bring to a simmer. Taste the soup for seasoning. I usually add another teaspoon or so of lemon juice. Simmer the soup very gently for another 2 minutes. If it is too thick, you can always thin it down with a little chicken stock or water.

Poppadum

Paapar

THESE THIN CRISP DISCS are sold, either plain or flavoured with spices and seasonings such as garlic, black pepper or red pepper. They are partially prepared. A seasoned dough made from dried pulses has already been rolled out into the required shapes and then dried in the sun. All that you have to do is cook the poppadum. The cooking process is quick and easy.

There are two basic methods to choose from. Deep-frying is the traditional method. This allows the poppadums to expand to their fullest and to turn very airy. It also brings out their full flavour. This method does, however, leave those who are nibbling the poppadum with slightly greasy fingers. The second method is to roast the poppadums directly over or under a flame. This way you end up with clean fingers and poppadums with fewer calories, but the poppadums do not expand as much and remain denser than fried ones.

Poppadums may be served with drinks or with Indian meals of any sort.

COOKING TIME: 4 minutes for each poppadum

Serves 6	*Serves 6*
Roasting method:	*Frying method:*
6 poppadums	*6 poppadums*
	vegetable oil for deep-frying

Roasting method:

1.	Heat your grill. Put 1 poppadum on a rack and place it about 5-7.5 cm (2-3 inches) below the grill. Now watch it very carefully. It will expand in seconds. It will also turn paler and develop a few bubbles. Turn it over and expose the second side to the flame for a second or so. Watch it all the time and do not let it brown or burn. Remove the poppadum from the grill. Grill all the poppadums this way.

2.	Poppadums may also be roasted directly on top of a live flame. Of course, you can only do this if you have a gas cooker. If you wish to follow this method, turn the flame to low. Now grip a poppadum with a set of tongs and hold it 1 cm (½ inch) above the flame. The part of the poppadum that is directly over the flame will bubble and turn lighter in colour. When that happens, expose another part of the poppadum to the flame. Keep doing this until the entire poppadum has been roasted.

Frying method:

1.	Depending upon the size of the poppadum either leave them whole or snap each one into two halves. Remember that they will expand in the frying pan.

2.	Put about 2 cm (¾ inch) of oil in a frying pan and set it to heat over a medium flame. When it is hot, put in 1 poppadum (or half a poppadum, depending upon the size of the frying pan and poppadum). It will sizzle and expand within seconds. Remove the poppadum with a slotted spoon and drain on a paper towel. cook all the poppadums in this way.

3.	Poppadums should retain their yellowish colour and not turn brown. They should cook very fast. Adjust the heat, if necessary.

*F*ried cashews

Tale huay caju

CASHEWS that have been freshly fried at home have an exquisite taste, far better than that of the canned and bottled variety. In India, this was the only kind of cashew we ate, with my mother frying the nuts just before my father sat down for his evening Scotch and soda.
Raw cashews can be bought at most health-food stores.

PREPARATION TIME: 2 minutes
COOKING TIME: 5-7 minutes

Serves 4-6
vegetable oil for deep-frying
225 g (8 oz) raw cashew nuts
¼ teaspoon salt
freshly ground black pepper

1.   Put a sieve on top of a metal bowl and set it near the stove. Also, line two plates with paper towels and set them nearby.
2.   Heat about 2.5 cm (1 inch) of oil in a deep 20 cm (8 inch) frying pan over a medium flame. When it is hot, put in all the cashews. Stir and fry them until they turn a reddish-gold colour. This happens fairly fast. Now empty the contents of the frying pan into the sieve to drain the oil. Lift up the sieve and shake out the extra oil. Spread the cashews out on one of the plates and sprinkle the salt and pepper on them. Stir to mix. Now slide the cashews on to the second plate. This will drain some more of the oil from them. Serve the cashews warm or after they have cooled.

From the left: Poppadum, Fried cashews

From the left: Skewered chicken kebabs; Lamb or beef kebabs

Lamb or beef kebabs

Boti kabab

THESE KEBABS make excellent nibbling fare for snacks.

PREPARATION TIME: 10 minutes, plus marinating
COOKING TIME: 10-12 minutes

Serves 4 as a snack
225-250 g (8-9 oz) boned lamb from shoulder or leg, or beef steak
4 tablespoons plain yogurt
1 ½ tablespoons lemon juice
1 × 2.5 cm (1 inch) cube of fresh ginger, peeled and very finely grated
1 garlic clove, peeled and crushed
1 teaspoon ground cumin
½ teaspoon ground coriander
¼ teaspoon cayenne pepper
¾ teaspoon salt
1 ½ tablespoons vegetable oil

1.   Cut the meat into 2 cm (¾ inch) cubes and put them into a non-metallic bowl.

2.   Combine the yogurt, lemon juice, ginger, garlic, cumin, coriander, cayenne and salt in a bowl and mix well. Hold a sieve over the meat and pour the yogurt mixture into it. Push the mixture through the sieve, extracting all the paste that you can. Mix the meat and the marinade well. Cover and refrigerate for 6-24 hours.

3.   Thread the meat on to skewers. Balance the ends of the skewers on the rim of a baking tray in such a way that all the meat juices drip inside the tray. Brush the kebabs generously with oil and place the baking tray under a preheated hot grill. When one side of the meat gets lightly browned, turn the skewers to brown the other side, making sure to brush this side first with more oil.

132

Skewered chicken kebabs

Murghi tikka

YOU COULD SERVE these pieces of marinated and baked chicken as a first course or you could cut them in halves, stick toothpicks in them and pass them around with drinks. It has become traditional in Indian restaurants, where *Murghi tikka* is offered before the main course, to arrange the chicken pieces prettily on a platter and then surround them with thickly cut slices of onions sautéed very lightly in oil, some sliced cucumbers and wedges of lime.

This dish belongs to the same family as tandoori chicken and should, ideally, be cooked in a *tandoor* or clay oven. I find that ordinary home ovens, heated to their maximum temperature, make adequate substitutes.

Murghi tikka is a useful dish to have in one's repertoire. Most of the work – and it is not much – can be done a day ahead of time. All that remains then is to brush the chicken pieces with butter and slip them into the oven for about 15 minutes.

PREPARATION TIME: 10 minutes, plus marinating
COOKING TIME: 15-20 minutes
OVEN: 240°C, 475°F, Gas Mark 9

Serves 4-6
6 chicken breasts, net weight after boning and skinning, about 1.25 kg (2¾ lb)
1¼ teaspoons salt
1 juicy lemon, halved
6 tablespoons plain yogurt
1 × 2.5 cm (1 inch) cube of fresh ginger, peeled and finely grated
3 garlic cloves, peeled and mashed to a pulp
1 teaspoon ground cumin
⅛-¼ teaspoon cayenne pepper
¼ teaspoon garam masala (page 13)
2 teaspoons yellow liquid food colouring mixed with ½ teaspoon red liquid food colouring
about 100 g (4 oz) unsalted butter, melted

1. Remove all the fat from the chicken pieces and cut each breast into 3-4 more or less equal pieces. Lay the pieces in a single layer on a platter. Sprinkle half the salt over them. Squeeze the juice from half the lemon over them as well. Rub the salt and lemon into the chicken. Turn the chicken pieces over and do the same on the other side with the remaining salt and lemon. Set aside for 20 minutes.

2. Meanwhile, put the yogurt into a small bowl. Beat it with a fork or whisk until it is smooth and creamy. Add the ginger, garlic, cumin, cayenne and garam masala. Stir to mix.

3. After the chicken has sat around in its first marinade for 20 minutes, brush one side with the food colouring. Turn the chicken pieces over with a pair of tongs and brush the other side with the colouring. Put the chicken pieces and all their accumulated juices into a bowl. Hold a sieve over the chicken pieces. Pour the yogurt mixture into the sieve and then push through as much of it as you can with a rubber spatula. Fold this second marinade over the chicken pieces. Cover tightly and refrigerate for 6-24 hours.

4. Thread the chicken pieces on to skewers, leaving a little space between each piece. Balance the skewers on the raised rim of a baking tray, making sure that the meat juices will drip on to the tray and not your oven floor. Brush the chicken with half the melted butter and put it in the oven for about 7 minutes. Take out the baking tray and the skewers. Turn the chicken pieces over and brush again with the butter. Bake for 8-10 minutes or until the chicken is just done. Do not overcook it.

Delicious cocktail koftas

Chhote kofte

ALMOST every country has some type of meatball. These Indian ones are made out of minced lamb and you can eat them as part of a meal or serve them as snacks.

PREPARATION TIME: 20 minutes   COOKING TIME: 25 minutes

Makes 30 meatballs and serves 6 for snacks, 4 for dinner
MEATBALLS:
450 g (1 lb) minced lamb
½ teaspoon salt
1 teaspoon ground cumin
1 teaspoon ground coriander
¼ teaspoon garam masala (page 13)
⅛ teaspoon cayenne pepper
2 tablespoons very finely chopped fresh coriander
3 tablespoons plain yogurt
SAUCE:
5 garlic cloves, peeled
2.5 cm (1 inch) cube of fresh ginger, peeled and coarsely chopped
4-5 tablespoons water, plus 300 ml (½ pint)
1 teaspoon ground cumin
1 teaspoon ground coriander
1 teaspoon bright red paprika
¼ teaspoon cayenne pepper
5 tablespoons vegetable oil
2.5 cm (1 inch) piece of cinnamon stick
6 cardamom pods
6 cloves
100 g (4 oz) onion, peeled and finely chopped
100 g (4 oz) tomato, peeled (page 18) and chopped, or use canned tomatoes
4 tablespoons plain yogurt
½ teaspoon salt

1.   Combine all the ingredients for the meatballs. Dip your hands in water whenever you need to and form about 30 meatballs.

2.   Make the sauce. Put the garlic and ginger into the container of a food processor with 4 tablespoons of water. Blend to a paste. Put the paste into a bowl. Add the cumin, ground coriander, paprika and cayenne. Stir to mix.

3.   Heat the oil in a heavy wide saucepan over a medium-high flame. When it is hot, put in the cinnamon, cardamom and cloves. Stir for 3-4 seconds. Now put in the onions and fry them, stirring all the time, until they are reddish-brown in colour. Turn the heat to medium and put in the paste from the bowl and the chopped tomato. Stir and fry this mixture until it turns a brownish colour.

4.   When it begins to catch, add 1 tablespoon of yogurt. Stir and fry some more until the yogurt is incorporated into the sauce. Now add another tablespoon of yogurt. Incorporate that into the sauce as well. Keep doing this until you have put in all the yogurt.

5.   Now put in the remaining water and ½ teaspoon salt. Stir and bring to a simmer. Put in all the meatballs in a single layer. Cover, leaving the lid very slightly open, turn the heat to low and cook for 25 minutes. Stir very gently, every 5 minutes or so.

6.   Towards the end of the cooking period, scrape the bottom of the pan just to make sure the sauce is not catching. If necessary, add a little water. Remove the lid and turn the heat up to medium low. Stir gently and cook until the meatballs look brown. The sauce should be clinging to the meatballs and there should be a little fat left at the bottom of the pan.

7.   When you are ready to eat, heat the koftas gently. Lift them out of the fat and shake off any whole spices that may be clinging to them. Stick a toothpick into each kofta if serving with drinks. If you have these koftas for dinner, you could leave more of a sauce.

Clockwise from top left: Delicious cocktail koftas;
Deep-fried stuffed savoury pastry (page 136);
Tandoori-style prawns (page 137);
Fresh coriander chutney (page 121)

Deep-fried stuffed savoury pastry

Samosa

SAMOSAS, generally eaten as a snack in India, make excellent appetizers. You may stuff them with almost anything, although traditional stuffings are either made out of spicy potatoes or ground meat. If you wish to use the ground meat stuffing, just use the recipe for Minced lamb with mint (page 24). Boil away the liquid and drain the fat. Stuff each samosa with about 2½ tablespoons of the cooked mince. Samosas may be eaten with Fresh coriander chutney (page 121) which serves as a dip.

Here is my recipe for samosas with the potato stuffing:

PREPARATION TIME: 1¼ hours, plus standing
COOKING TIME: 20-25 minutes

Makes 16
PASTRY:
225 g (8 oz) plain flour
½ teaspoon salt
4 tablespoons vegetable oil, plus a little extra
4-5 tablespoons water
STUFFING:
750 g (1½ lb) potatoes, boiled in their jackets and allowed to cool
4 tablespoons vegetable oil
1 medium onion, peeled and finely chopped
175 g (6 oz) shelled peas
1 tablespoon finely grated peeled fresh ginger
1 fresh hot green chilli, finely chopped
3 tablespoons very finely chopped fresh coriander
3-4 tablespoons water
1½ teaspoons salt – or to taste
1 teaspoon ground coriander
1 teaspoon garam masala (page 13)
1 teaspoon ground roasted cumin seeds (page 13)
¼ teaspoon cayenne pepper
2 tablespoons lemon juice
vegetable oil for deep-frying

1. Sift the flour and salt into a bowl. Add the 4 tablespoons of vegetable oil and rub it in with your fingers until the mixture resembles coarse breadcrumbs. Slowly add about 4 tablespoons water – or a tiny bit more – and gather the dough into a stiff ball.

2. Empty the ball out on to a clean work surface. Knead the dough for about 10 minutes or until it is smooth. Make a ball. Rub the ball with about ¼ teaspoon of the oil and slip it into a polythene bag. Set it aside for 30 minutes or longer.

3. Make the stuffing. Peel the potatoes and cut them into 5 mm (¼ inch) dice. Heat 4 tablespoons of oil in a large frying pan over a medium flame. When it is hot, put in the onions. Stir and fry them until they begin to turn brown at the edges. Add the peas, ginger, green chilli, fresh coriander and 3 tablespoons of water. Cover, lower the heat and simmer until the peas are cooked. Stir every now and then and add a little more water if the frying pan seems to dry out.

4. Add the diced potatoes, salt, coriander, garam masala, roasted cumin, cayenne and lemon juice. Stir to mix. Cook on a low heat for 3-4 minutes, stirring gently as you do so. Check the balance of salt and lemon juice. You may want more of both. Turn off the heat and allow the mixture to cool.

5. Knead the pastry dough again and divide it into 8 balls. Keep 7 covered while you work with the eighth. Roll this ball out into an 18 cm (7 inch) round. Cut it in half with a sharp pointed knife. Pick up one half and form a cone, making a 5 mm (¼ inch) wide, overlapping seam. Fasten this seam together with a

little water. Fill the cone with about 2½ tablespoons of the potato mixture. Close the top of the cone by sealing the open edges together with a little water. Again, your seam should be about 5 mm (¼ inch) wide. Press the top seam down with the prongs of a fork or flute it with your fingers. Make 15 more samosas.

6.   Heat about 4-5 cm (1½-2 inches) of oil for deep-frying over a medium-low flame. You may use a small deep frying pan for this or an Indian *karhai*. When the oil is medium-hot, put in as many samosas as the pan will hold in a single layer. Fry slowly, turning the samosas frequently until they are golden brown and crisp. Drain on paper towels and serve hot, warm or at room temperature.

The flower gatherers, Basoli, Kashmir, late 19th century

*T*andoori-style prawns

Tandoori jhinga

THESE marinated prawns are traditionally cooked in a *tandoor*. Since the prawns generally available in Britain tend to be small, I cook them very quickly in a frying pan. You may easily double the recipe, if you wish to serve these prawns as a main course. Just use a larger frying pan.

PREPARATION TIME: 5 minutes, plus marinating
COOKING TIME: 7 minutes

Serves 4 as a snack
4 tablespoons plain yogurt
1×2.5 cm (1 inch) cube of fresh ginger, peeled and very finely grated
1 large garlic clove, peeled and mashed to a pulp
5 teaspoons lemon juice
¼ teaspoon salt, or to taste
freshly ground black pepper
1½ teaspoons ground roasted cumin seeds (page 13)
¼ teaspoon garam masala (page 13)
2 teaspoons yellow liquid food colouring mixed with 1 teaspoon red liquid food colouring
225 g (8 oz) good quality peeled prawns, thawed (if frozen) and patted dry
50 g (2 oz) unsalted butter

1.   Put the yogurt into a bowl. Beat lightly with a fork or a whisk until it is smooth and creamy. Add the ginger, garlic, lemon juice, salt, some black pepper, roasted cumin, garam masala and the liquid food colouring. Stir to mix and set aside for 15 minutes. Push this liquid through a sieve into a second bowl. Add the prawns to the marinade and mix well. Set aside for 30 minutes. Remove the prawns with a slotted spoon, leaving all the marinade behind in the bowl.

2.   Melt the butter in a 20-23 cm (8-9 inch) frying pan over a medium flame. When the butter has melted completely, turn the heat to medium-high and immediately pour in the marinade. Stir and fry for a few minutes or until the butter separates and you have a thick bubbly sauce clinging to the bottom of the pan. Add the prawns and fold them in. Cook for a few minutes, stirring gently. Do not overcook the prawns.

3.   Stick cocktail sticks in the prawns and serve them immediately.

Spicy matchstick potato crisps

Aloo ka tala hua laccha

THIS IS one of those snack foods that Indians munch noisily while watching Indian movie epics in which bandits chase weeping, but upstanding heroines and scantily clad girls shake their hips at the dashing heroes.

PREPARATION TIME: 15 minutes COOKING TIME: 30-40 minutes

Serves 4-6 with drinks
100 g (4 oz) onion, peeled and coarsely chopped
2-3 garlic cloves, peeled
1 dried hot red chilli (use more if you want the potatoes to be more than mildly hot)
1 teaspoon ground cumin
½ teaspoon ground coriander
450 g (1 lb) potatoes
enough vegetable oil to have a 1 cm (½ inch) layer in a big frying pan
¾-1 teaspoon salt

1. Put the onion, garlic and red chilli into the container of an electric blender or food processor. Blend until you have a paste, pushing down with a rubber spatula, if necessary. Empty the paste into a bowl. Add the cumin and coriander and mix them in.
2. Peel the potatoes and cut them into 3 mm (⅛ inch) thick slices. You may use a mandoline, food processor or knife to do this. Stack about 5 slices together at a time and cut them into 3 mm (⅛ inch) wide matchsticks. (You can either fry the potatoes as soon as they are cut or else leave them to soak in water and pat them dry.)
3. Line one very large or two smaller platters with paper towels and set them in a convenient place near the cooker.
4. Heat about 1 cm (½ inch) of oil in a deep 25-30 cm (10-12 inch) frying pan over a medium flame. When it is hot, put in as many of the cut potatoes as the pan will hold easily without overcrowding. Stir and fry until the potatoes are golden and crisp. Remove the potatoes with a slotted spoon and spread them out on the platter. Fry all the potatoes this way, spreading out each batch on the paper towels.

5. Take the frying pan off the heat and remove all but 4 tablespoons of the oil. Put the frying pan back on the medium flame and pour in the spice mixture. Stir and fry it until it is brown and fairly dry. Take your time doing this, turning the heat down a bit if you think it is necessary. Now put in all the fried potatoes and the salt. Stir to mix, breaking up the spice lumps as you do so. Drain again and serve.

Semolina halva

Sooji ka halva

THIS VERY LIGHT, fluffy halva may be eaten as a snack or at the end of a meal.

PREPARATION TIME: 5 minutes
COOKING TIME: 25 minutes

Serves 6
600 ml (1 pint) water
5 tablespoons vegetable oil or ghee (page 13)
25 g (1 oz) slivered, blanched almonds
300 g (11 oz) fine-grained semolina
165 g (5½ oz) sugar
2-3 tablespoons sultanas
¼ teaspoon finely crushed cardamom seeds (use a pestle and mortar)

1. Put 600 ml (1 pint) of water to boil in a saucepan. Once it comes to a rolling boil, turn the heat down to very low and let the saucepan sit on the back of the cooker.
2. Heat the oil or ghee in a large, preferably non-stick, frying pan over a medium flame. When it is hot, put in the almonds. Stir

138

From the top: Spicy matchstick potato crisps;
Semolina halva; Carrot halva

and fry them until they turn golden. Take them out with a slotted spoon and leave them to drain on paper towels. Put the semolina into the same oil. Turn the heat to medium-low. Now stir and gently fry the semolina for 8-10 minutes or until it turns a warm, golden colour. Do not let it brown.

3.   Add the sugar to the pan and stir it in.

4.   Very slowly pour the boiling water into the pan. Keep stirring as you do so. Take a good 2 minutes to do this. When all the water has been added, turn the heat to low. Stir and cook the halva for 5 minutes. Add the sultanas, almonds and crushed cardamom seeds. Stir and cook the halva for another 5 minutes.

5.   This halva may be served hot or warm or at room temperature.

Carrot halva

Gajar ka halva

PREPARATION TIME: 10 minutes
COOKING TIME: about 1¼ hours

Serves 4

450 g (1 lb) carrots, peeled and grated

750 ml (1¼ pints) milk

8 cardamom pods

5 tablespoons vegetable oil or ghee
(page 16)

5 tablespoons caster sugar

1-2 tablespoons sultanas

1 tablespoon shelled, unsalted pistachios,
lightly crushed

300 ml (½ pint) clotted or double cream
(optional)

1.   Put the grated carrots, milk and carda-mom pods in a heavy-based saucepan and bring to a boil. Turn the heat to medium and cook, stirring now and then, until there is no liquid left. Adjust the heat, if you need to. This boiling down of the milk will take at least 1 hour, depending upon the width of your pan.

2.   Heat the oil or ghee in a non-stick frying pan over a medium-low flame. When it is hot, put in the carrot mixture. Stir and fry until the carrots no longer have a wet, milky look. They should turn a rich, reddish colour. This can take 10-15 minutes.

3.   Add the sugar, sultanas and pistachios. Stir and fry for another 2 minutes.

4.   This halva may be served warm or at room temperature. Serve the cream on the side for those who want it.

*I*ce cream with nuts

Kulfi

AS FAR AS I CAN REMEMBER, we never made *kulfi* at home. This may well have been because it was served always to hundreds of people at wedding banquets. Only a professional *kulfi-wallah* could be entrusted with such a monstrous task. Orders were placed with him weeks in advance. On the day of the banquet, he arrived with assistants, usually his sons and brothers, carrying enormous earthenware vats. The vats were set up somewhere outdoors, usually at the edge of a vast lawn.
Each vat contained lots of broken ice and, embedded in the ice, hundreds of tube-shaped terra-cotta containers filled with *kulfi*. Every now and then the *kulfi-wallah* would ease his arm into the vats and give its contents a knowing swish. We were never allowed to ask for a *kulfi* until the main meal, set up under brightly appliquéd tents, had finished.
Kulfi is not difficult to make at home as I have discovered in the years that I have been deprived of local *kulfi-wallahs*. All you need is an adequate freezer. (If any of you have an ice cream machine, you may use it for *kulfi*.) *Kulfi* is not made with cream but with reduced milk. It helps to have a very heavy pan with an even distribution of heat for boiling down the milk. A heavy, non-stick saucepan would do.

PREPARATION TIME: 5 minutes, plus cooling and freezing
COOKING TIME: about 1 ¼ hours

Serves 6
2 litres (3½ pints) milk
10 cardamom pods
4-5 tablespoons sugar
15 g (½ oz) blanched almonds, chopped
25 g (1 oz) unsalted pistachios, shelled and chopped

1.   Bring the milk to the boil in a heavy saucepan. As soon as the milk begins to rise, turn the heat down, adjusting it to allow the milk to simmer vigorously without boiling over. Add the cardamom pods. The milk has to reduce to about one-third of its original quantity, that is, to about 750 ml (1 ¼ pints). Stir frequently as this happens. Whenever a film forms on top of the milk, just stir it in.
2.   When the milk has reduced, remove the cardamom pods and discard them. Add the sugar and almonds. Stir and simmer gently for 2-3 minutes. Pour the reduced milk into a bowl and let it cool completely. Add half the pistachios and stir them in. Cover the bowl with aluminium foil and put it in the freezer.
3.   Put 6 small freezerproof dishes, empty yogurt cartons or a 900 ml (1½ pint) pudding basin into the refrigerator to chill.
4.   Every 15 minutes or so remove the ice cream bowl from the freezer and give the *kulfi* a good stir in order to break up the crystals. As the *kulfi* begins to freeze, it will become harder and harder to stir. When it becomes almost impossible to stir, take the containers out of the refrigerator. Work quickly now. Divide the *kulfi* between the dishes or empty it into the pudding basin. Sprinkle the remaining pistachios over the top. Cover the dishes or basin with aluminium foil, crinkling the edges to seal them. Put the kulfi into the freezer and let it harden.

Krishna and Radha, Northern Indian painting, late 19th century

From the left: Ice cream with nuts; Spiced tea

Spiced tea

Masala chai

THIS TEA, flavoured with cinnamon, cardamom and cloves may be served at tea time or at the end of a meal. I love it on cold blustery days with some Spicy matchstick potato crisps (page 138) to nibble on the side.

PREPARATION TIME: 2 minutes
COOKING TIME: 15 minutes

Serves 2
600 ml (1 pint) water
2.5 cm (1 inch) piece of cinnamon stick
8 cardamom pods
8 cloves
175 ml (6 fl oz) milk
6 teaspoons sugar, or to taste
3 teaspoons unperfumed, loose black tea

1.   Put the water into a saucepan. Add the cinnamon, cardamom and cloves and bring to a boil. Cover, turn the heat to low and simmer for 10 minutes. Add the milk and sugar and bring to a simmer again. Throw in the tea leaves, cover, and turn off the heat. After 2 minutes, strain the tea into cups and serve them immediately.

INDEX

INDEX

ACKNOWLEDGEMENTS

The publishers thank the following for
providing the photographs and
illustrations in this book:
Art Director's Photo Library 9; Baldev/
Transworld Features 6; Bridgeman Art
Library (British Museum) 115, (India
Office Library) 125 above, (Victoria and
Albert Museum) 120; ET Archive
(Victoria and Albert Museum) 120; ET
Archive (Victoria and Albert Museum)
37, 87, 137, 140; Greg Evans Photo
Library 8; Format/Margaret Murray 17;
Susan Griggs Agency (John Blaustein)
96-7; (Jehangir Gazdar) 126-7, (Robin
Laurance) 64, (Patrick Ward) 7; Sunil
Gupta/Network 96; Michael Holford
(Victoria and Albert Museum) 42, 58;
Michael McIntyre/Hutchison Library
74-5; Rex Features 103; Alastair Scott
64-5; Tony Stone Associates 75; Sara
Taylor 10, 15, 22-3, 44-5, 88, 116;
Zefa Picture Library 1, 102-3.

Food photographer: Sara Taylor
Stylists: Sarah Wiley and Tessa Rosier
Food prepared for photography by Jennie
    Shapter and Clare Gordon Smith
Indian photographic
    consultant: Shehzad Husain
Chapter openers: Jane Brewster